Focus on Grammar and Meaning

Oxford Key Concepts for the Language Classroom series

Focus on Assessment
Eunice Eunhee Jang

Focus on Content-Based Language Teaching
Patsy M. Lightbown

Focus on Grammar and Meaning
Luciana C. de Oliveira and Mary J. Schleppegrell

Focus on Literacy
Danling Fu and Marylou M. Matoush

Focus on Oral Interaction
Rhonda Oliver and Jenefer Philp

Focus on Grammar and Meaning

Luciana C. de Oliveira and Mary J. Schleppegrell

OXFORD
UNIVERSITY PRESS

OXFORD
UNIVERSITY PRESS

Great Clarendon Street, Oxford, OX2 6DP,
United Kingdom

Oxford University Press is a department of the
University of Oxford.
It furthers the University's objective of excellence in
research, scholarship,and education by publishing
worldwide. Oxford is a registered trade mark of
Oxford University Press in the UK and in certain
other countries

ISBN: 978 0 19 400085 7

Printed in China

This book is printed on paper from certified and
well-managed sources

ACKNOWLEDGMENTS

*The authors and publisher are grateful to those who have given permission
to reproduce the following extracts and adaptations of copyright
material*: pp.4, 77–8 Extracts from *Officer Buckle and Gloria* by
Peggy Rathmann, copyright © 1995 by Peggy Rathmann. Used
by permission of G. P. Putnam's Sons Books for Young Readers, a
division of Penguin Group (USA) LLC. pp.13, 69, 77 Extracts from
Scott Foresman Science, http://pearsonkt.com. Copyright © Pearson
Education, Inc., or its affiliates. Used by permission. All Rights
Reserved. pp.32–3 Extracts from "Three functions of output in
second language learning" by Merrill Swain from *Principle and
Practice in Applied Linguistics: Studies in Honour of H. G. Widdowson*

edited by Guy Cook and Barbara Seidlhofer, Oxford University
Press, 1995. Reproduced by permission of Oxford University
Press. p.39 Extract from "The role of focus-on-forms tasks in
promoting child L2 acquisition" by Birgit Harley in *Focus on
form in classroom second language acquisition* by Catherine Doughty
and Jessica Williams (eds.), Cambridge University Press, 1998.
© Cambridge University Press, reproduced with permission.
p.40 Extract from *Julius* by Angela Johnson. Scholastic Inc./
Orchard Books. Copyright © 1993 by Angela Johnson. Used by
permission. pp.48, 68 Excerpt from "Settling Alta California"
from *Harcourt Brace Social Studies*, Student Edition, Grade 4.
Copyright © 2000 by Harcourt, Inc. Reproduced by permission of
the publisher, Houghton Mifflin Harcourt Publishing Company.
pp.48, 90, 92 Reprinted from *Journal of English for Academic Purposes*,
Volume 5 (4), Mary J. Schleppegrell and Luciana C. de Oliveira,
"An integrated language and content approach for history
teachers", Copyright 2006, with permission from Elsevier. pp.54,
65–7 Figure and extracts © Pauline Gibbons, 2006, *Bridging
Discourses in the ESL Classroom: Students, Teachers and Researchers*,
Bloomsbury Continuum, an imprint of Bloomsbury Publishing
Plc. p.63 Table from "The Role of Metalanguage in Supporting
Academic Language Development" by Mary J. Schleppegrell,
Language Learning, Volume 63 (1), March 2013. © 2013 Language
Learning Research Club, University of Michigan. Reproduced
by permission of John Wiley and Sons. p.72 Extract republished
with permission of Sage Publications, Inc. Books, from *Formative
Assessment for Literacy, Grades K–6: Building Reading and Academic
Language Skills Across the Curriculum* by Alison L. Bailey and Margaret
Heritage (eds.), 2008; permission conveyed through Copyright
Clearance Center, Inc. pp.74–5 Table adapted from "Beyond
General Strategies for English Language Learners: Language
Dissection in Science" by Luciana C. de Oliveira and Kathryn
N. Dodds, The Electronic Journal of Literacy Through Science,
Volume 9 (1), 2010. Reproduced by permission of *Electronic Journal
of Literacy through Science*. p.81 Table adapted from © Frances
Christie and Beverly Derewianka, 2010, *School Discourse: Learning
to Write Across the Years of Schooling*, Bloomsbury Continuum, an
imprint of Bloomsbury Publishing Plc. pp.81–2 Figures reprinted
from *Journal of Second Language Writing*, Volume 25, Luciana C.
de Oliveira and Shu-Wen Lan, "Writing science in an upper
elementary classroom: A genre-based approach to teaching
English language learners", Copyright 2014, with permission
from Elsevier. p.90 Extract from "The Grammar of History:
Enhancing Content-Based Instruction Through a Functional
Focus on Language" by Mary J. Schleppegrell, Mariana Achugar
and Teresa Oteíza, *TESOL Quarterly*, Volume 38 (1), 2004. © 2004
TESOL International Association. Reproduced by permission
of John Wiley and Sons. pp.91, 95–6 Excerpts from *Modern
World History: Patterns of Interaction*, Student Edition. Copyright
© 2007 by McDougal Littell Inc. All rights reserved. Reprinted
by permission of the publisher, Houghton Mifflin Harcourt
Publishing Company. pp.93–4 Extract from *America: Pathways to
the Present Modern Student Edition 2002C Fourth Edition* by Andrew
Cayton, Elisabeth I. Perry, Linda Reed and Allan M Winkler
Copyright © 2002 Pearson Education, Inc., or its affiliates. Used
by permission. All Rights Reserved. p.98 Figures reprinted from
Journal of Second Language Writing, Volume 16 (4), Pamela Spycher,
"Academic writing of adolescent English learners: Learning to
use 'although'", Copyright 2007, with permission from Elsevier.
pp.102, 105 Extracts from *The Roles of Language in CLIL* by Ana
Llinares, Tom Morton and Rachel Whittaker (2012). © Cambridge
University Press 2012, reproduced by kind permission of the
authors and Cambridge University Press. p.104 Extract from "'It
was taught good and I learned a lot': Intellectual practices and
ESL learners in the middle years" by Pauline Gibbons, *Australian
Journal of Language and Literacy*, Volume 31 (2), 2008. Reproduced
by permission of the Australian Literacy Educators' Association.
p.106 Extract reprinted from *System*, Volume 37 (3), Sarah J. Shin,
"Negotiating Grammatical Choices: Academic Language Learning
by Secondary ESL Students", Copyright 2009, with permission
from Elsevier. p.108 Extracts from "Using Systemic-Functional
Linguistics in Content and Language Integrated Learning"
by Rachel Whittaker, *NALDIC Quarterly*, Volume 8 (1), 2010.
Reproduced by permission of NALDIC.

Sources: *History Alive! The Medieval World and Beyond* by Bert Bower
(Teachers Curriculum Institute, 2004). *Urban Roosts: Where Birds
Nest in the City* by Barbara Bash (Little, Brown and Company, 1992).

*To the teachers and students who have helped us develop this
focus on grammar and meaning, and to Michael Halliday,
whose functional grammar inspires us.*

Contents

Contents

Acknowledgments

In writing this book, we have gained much inspiration and knowledge from the work of many researchers who have studied issues related to grammar instruction, and specifically functional grammar. We have also learned a great deal from the teachers and educators with whom we have worked over many years who have applied functional grammar activities in their classrooms. We are also grateful to our students who helped us shape much of the work that appears in this text. Many of their names appear in the book and in the reference list.

We are grateful to Oxford University Press, especially to Sophie Rogers and Julia Bell for their support and attention to detail. We would like to thank Patsy Lightbown and Nina Spada for the invitation to write this book and to contribute to their valuable series, and for their feedback on our chapters and support throughout the process.

We are also grateful to Alex and John for their patience and continued encouragement as we traveled to complete this project and spent many weekends and precious hours finalizing it.

Series Editors' Preface

The Oxford Key Concepts for the Language Classroom series is designed to provide accessible information about research on topics that are important to second language teachers. Each volume focuses on a particular area of second/foreign-language learning and teaching, covering both background research and classroom-based studies. The emphasis is on how knowing about this research can guide teachers in their instructional planning, pedagogical activities, and assessment of learners' progress.

The idea for the series was inspired by the book *How Languages are Learned*. Many colleagues have told us that they appreciate the way that book can be used either as part of a university teacher education program or in a professional development course for experienced teachers. They have commented on the value of publications that show teachers and future teachers how knowing about research on language learning and teaching can help them think about their own teaching principles and practices.

This series is oriented to the educational needs and abilities of school-aged children (5–18 years old) with distinct chapters focusing on research that is specific to primary- and secondary-level learners. The volumes are written for second language teachers, whether their students are minority-language speakers learning the majority language or students learning a foreign language in a classroom far from the communities where the language is spoken. Some of the volumes will be useful to 'mainstream' teachers who have second language learners among their students, but have limited training in second/foreign language teaching. Some of the volumes will also be primarily for teachers of English, whereas others will be of interest to teachers of other languages as well.

The series includes volumes on topics that are key for second language teachers of school-age children and each volume is written by authors whose research and teaching experience have focused on learners and teachers in this age group. While much has been written about some of these topics, most publications are either 'how to' methodology texts with no explicit link to research, or academic works that are designed for researchers and postgraduate students who require a thorough scholarly treatment of the research, rather than an overview and interpretation for classroom practice. Instructors in programs for teachers often find that the methodology texts lack the academic background appropriate for a university course and that the scholarly works are too long, too difficult, or not sufficiently classroom-oriented for the needs of teachers and future teachers. The volumes in this series are intended to bridge that gap.

The books are enriched by the inclusion of *Spotlight Studies* that represent important research and *Classroom Snapshots* that provide concrete examples of teaching/learning events in the second language classroom. In addition, through a variety of activities, readers will be able to integrate this information with their own experiences of learning and teaching.

Introduction

This is a book about a different kind of grammar teaching than you may be expecting. It doesn't provide grammar rules, doesn't offer advice about how to present particular grammar points or a pedagogy for explaining grammar, and there is little focus on learner errors and how to correct them. These aspects of grammar teaching are addressed in many other resources for teachers.

In this book, we introduce a functional grammar approach that adds to traditional grammar teaching in ways that fit with today's L2 teaching contexts. In our schools today, children typically learn a second language while also learning something else. Whether in communicative or content-based classrooms, children are usually learning the new language in order to engage in the tasks of the school curriculum, read texts at their age levels, and write in ways that will be valued.

This book offers a reconceptualization of how grammar teaching can support the L2 learning of children in the primary and secondary years of schooling. It draws on theories of language learning as well as recent research in L2 classrooms to describe grammar teaching in the context of and in service to the broader learning goals that we have for children in school. The reconceptualization extends to what grammar means, what its place in the school curriculum should be, and what we might consider the learning of grammar to consist of.

Many L2 learners are in classrooms with others at different levels of proficiency in the target language, and often also with native speakers of that language. Teachers need ways of supporting language learning and an approach to grammar that can be implemented with such diverse populations. Traditional grammar teaching cannot address the needs of all students in a classroom on an equal basis, as instruction on particular points of grammar will inevitably serve only students who make errors with those structures.

We offer an alternative approach that enables learners to reflect on language forms and meanings relevant to their particular stages of development. The focus is on structures relevant to curricular learning more generally, enabling all students to apply the new knowledge at their current proficiency levels in the tasks they engage in. We draw on the theory of functional grammar to move beyond thinking of grammar as rules to viewing it as a resource for meaning-making. Every language has a vast set of grammatical resources that speakers and writers can exploit. We see the role of the grammar teacher as supporting learners in drawing on a larger potential from the resources of the target language and extending their ability to participate in a wider range of activities using the language.

Functional grammar offers a way of thinking about language and structure not as a set of individual items to be learned and put together, but instead as meaningful segments that work together in sentences and discourse to make meaning. This puts a focus on the larger systems of the language as a whole. By connecting the forms and meanings to those larger systems of the grammar, we make the potential of the language more available to the learner.

For children learning additional languages via subject-matter instruction in schools, the priority has to be supporting them in the content learning they are expected to do. Without that, L2 learners can slowly fall behind as they miss out on the grade-level content that their peers are engaged with. L2 learners need consistent support for engaging with language in the curriculum contexts they encounter. The activities presented here are designed to be infused into content teaching and to support content learning. Our approach to grammar instruction calls on the teacher to identify language features and structures that are prominent in the texts children read and need to write, and to focus on those features and structures as a means of supporting children's learning more generally while also helping them see how the new language works. We offer examples of and guidance toward making language a topic of discussion, using meaningful grammatical metalanguage (language about language) to support the focus on form and meaning, and situating talk about language in the service of exploring how meaning is made in text and discourse. This approach to grammar teaching can expand students' capacity to make form–meaning connections and to recognize how the language being learned means what it does.

This book will get you started using a functional grammar approach in your content teaching. We hope it will stimulate your thinking about what grammar can be, motivate you to learn more about language and develop new ways of talking about it, and encourage you to make exploration of language a key component of all of your second language teaching.

1

Grammar and Meaning

Preview

Grammar teaching is a controversial topic. In fact, there is a lot of disagreement among researchers and teachers about the role of grammar in language learning and about the best approaches to teaching grammar. That is in part because there is disagreement about what 'grammar' itself means. Some see grammar as a set of rules that have to be followed, while others see it as a resource for meaning-making. We will explore both of these perspectives in this chapter.

Teachers may have strong affective reactions even to the word 'grammar', as our ideas about teaching grammar often come from our experiences: whether we had positive experiences of grammar learning and how we feel when we get **feedback** on the ways we talk or write. Some people love learning the rules and patterns in language and enjoy dissecting language to explore how it means what it does. Others see it as a tedious task requiring memorization of rules and exceptions.

Grammar instruction calls for specialized language that enables us to talk about language. Useful **metalanguage**, language for talking about language, will be introduced as we look into classrooms where students are engaged in talk about language and **content**. We will present studies that help us understand how best to focus on language form and meaning, and will offer examples of how to implement the research findings in classroom activities. We will demonstrate that, even without a lot of technical knowledge, teachers can explore grammar with their students, help them recognize how a language works, and learn new ways of using it.

Read Classroom Snapshots 1.1 and 1.2. Do you recognize these as examples of grammar teaching? What grammar is being taught? What metalanguage is being used? What are students learning through the interaction presented in the snapshots?

Classroom Snapshot 1.1

This transcript comes from a Grade 2 classroom in the USA. The students speak Arabic only or both Arabic and English as home languages and have a range of proficiency levels in English. The teacher wants to help children see that there are different ways people make statements or offers, ask questions, and give commands (what she refers to as different **speech functions**). She introduces them to three different grammatical **mood** options in English (**declarative, interrogative, imperative**) and asks them to think about these different ways of accomplishing the speech functions. The context for the activity is a story from the grade-level **Language Arts** program, *Officer Buckle and Gloria* by Peggy Rathmann. As it is about a police officer who gives safety lectures in schools, it contains many examples of commands, like 'Keep your shoelaces tied' and 'Never stand on a swivel chair' (Rathmann, 1995, no page numbers). The teacher has drawn up a chart that introduces the three grammatical moods and the four speech functions. She has assigned sentences from the story to the students, asking them to identify the mood and speech function in the context of the story, and put the sentence in the appropriate place on the chart.

Examples from the chart the teacher is developing:

'Commanding' in different ways

Declarative: 'I'd like someone to close the door'
Interrogative: 'Can you give me a command?'; 'Would you please sit right?'
Imperative: 'Keep your shoelaces tied'; 'Always wipe up spills before someone slips and falls'

As you read this transcript, keep the following questions in mind:
- What grammatical metalanguage are the teacher and students using?
- Is the metalanguage being used in meaningful ways?
- What do you think about the teacher's response to Hussein when he says, 'you just said one'?
- Do the children seem to be engaged and interested?
- Are the students learning grammar?

Teacher:	What's a command, Hassan?
Hassan:	It's like when, it's like when you are telling something like go to your room.
Teacher:	Right. This is the one we know mostly: 'Go to your room', 'Don't do this', 'Don't do that'. Hussein, do you know a command? Can you give me a command?
Hussein:	Well, you just said one.
Teacher:	Mmhmm. Did I give you a command?
Students:	[calling out responses] Yeah=

=No, you didn't give us a command=
=Yeah.

Teacher: I did?

Students: Yeah, you did.

Teacher: What kind of command?

Students: Give me a command=
=Question=
=Give me a question.

Teacher: Oh, did I give you a command?

Students: Yeah.=
=No.

Teacher: What kind of command is that?

Students: A question.

Teacher: Oh, I'm interrogating. Okay, did I give you a command?

Students: [all] Yeah.

(Schleppegrell, 2013, p. 159)

In Classroom Snapshot 1.1, the teacher herself is still learning to use the metalanguage of speech function and grammatical mood, and has to think about Hussein's unexpected response when he says, 'Well, you just said one'. This is not a conversation about what is 'correct'; instead, it is asking children to categorize sentences in a story to think about how the author creates the characters and how the characters interact. While the focus is on language forms, the discussion is about the meaning of those forms: whether 'can you give me a command?' is in fact a command. The class goes on to talk about who can command whom and the way we command some people in more polite ways than others. In the end, the teacher links the discussion back to the story and the children write their own commands in the form of safety tips like those in the story.

Conversations like this are supportive of second language development in several ways. First, the students are focusing on particular examples in order to recognize patterns in language, connecting form—the different mood choices—with function—giving commands—and recognizing that they can use different forms for the same function. They are also learning about **language variation**: that they can make choices about how to command, and that different choices are appropriate for different purposes. Finally, the metalanguage supports curricular learning, as students recognize how language choices contribute to the meaning of a literary text, an important goal of English Language Arts. Grammar is being learned here, but other things are also being learned, and the grammar is taught as a means of providing students with a way of talking about the author's language in meaningful ways.

This snapshot also illustrates another important feature of grammar teaching that will be highlighted across this volume. Research in second language development is clear about the important role of interaction in meaningful contexts in supporting language learning (see Oliver & Philp, 2014), and that holds true in grammar teaching. When children are engaged, as the children in Classroom Snapshot 1.1 are, in thinking about and responding to questions about the meaning of the language forms they are encountering, we can be confident that language learning is taking place.

Let's look at another example of the kind of grammar teaching you will be learning about in this book, this time from the secondary school classroom.

Classroom Snapshot 1.2

This example comes from a middle school classroom in California, where the students are working with a passage from their history textbook. The teacher is helping the students think about how history texts talk about **agency** (who is doing what to whom) by analyzing key sentences. In addition, she supports them in understanding how the language introduces and tracks concepts.

The teacher has developed a guiding question for this unit on Ancient Rome to focus students on the big ideas that they need to be thinking about as they read. Her question is, 'What were the internal weaknesses of the Roman Empire?' (Schleppegrell, Greer, & Taylor, 2008, p. 179). The class is looking closely at these sentences:

> To finance Rome's huge armies, its citizens had to pay heavy taxes. These taxes hurt the economy and drove many people into poverty.
>
> (Frey, 2005, p. 8)

The teacher wants students to understand that the heavy taxes used to support armies became an 'internal weakness' of the Roman Empire. She realizes that helping them explore the meaning in these sentences will assist them with this goal. She tells students to look at each verb and ask, 'Who or what is doing this?'. The students see that to understand who is 'acting' in 'To finance Rome's huge armies', they need to look ahead, as the agent of 'to finance' isn't named until the next clause, which begins with 'its citizens'.

The students identify 'its citizens' as the agents of 'financing Rome's huge armies' and 'paying heavy taxes'. The teacher asks what 'its' refers to, and helps the students see that 'its' refers to 'Rome's citizens'. They continue the discussion along these lines, identifying 'These taxes' as the same as 'heavy taxes' and recognizing that the agent of 'hurt the economy and drove many people into poverty' is 'taxes'.

The teacher then asks, 'Why would Rome need a huge army? How did the need for this army affect Roman citizens?' (Schleppegrell et al., 2008, p. 181). ▪

In Classroom Snapshot 1.2, we see how a focus on grammar can be meaningful and embedded in subject-matter teaching. This discussion helped students understand how English works in presenting agency, and in making links between different parts of a sentence and between different ways of referring to the same thing. Agency is an important concept in history, where teachers want students to think about who is presented as acting on others or being acted upon, among other things. In this case, teasing apart the way that the two parts of the sentence 'To finance Rome's huge armies, its citizens had to pay heavy taxes' are related to each other— with 'its citizens' being positioned as responsible for financing the armies— helps the students build understanding of the text. This, in turn, enables them to answer the questions about the Roman army that the teacher wants them to think about. Asking students to identify that the 'its' in the noun group 'its citizens' refers to 'Roman citizens' focuses them on how English uses pronouns and builds their knowledge about **reference** in English. These kinds of questions are examples of grammar teaching that supports students' content learning and prepares them to understand challenging historical concepts such as *internal weaknesses* in a civilization and how internal weaknesses are related to a civilization's rise or fall. Students can now answer the teacher's questions—'Why would Rome need a huge army? How did the need for this army affect Roman citizens?'—because they have developed their content understanding based on the language analysis. These questions show the teacher's goal of focusing on the overall meaning from the text. The discussion about language supported students' understanding and was followed by a richer conversation about internal weaknesses than the class could otherwise have had. In addition, the teacher found that this **scaffolding** enabled students to begin to recognize independently how agency is presented and how concepts are introduced and developed by an author. In this way, grammar teaching prepared students to better understand and think more critically about history by applying similar strategies to the language of other texts. At the same time, they were learning about how English works.

What Is Grammar Teaching?

Language teachers also further their understanding about grammar teaching from research. This book presents some different ways grammar has been investigated by researchers and taught by teacher-researchers around the world. It will offer insights into how the teaching and learning of grammar can contribute to learning a **second** or **foreign language**, and show how students can develop grammatical knowledge as they learn academic subjects. We will explore ways in which the research presented here can inform and enlighten us as we work with second language learners to improve their language **proficiency**. Before we begin our exploration of the research, take a few minutes to reflect on what you think about grammar teaching.

Activity 1.1

The statements below represent views that some people hold about grammar teaching. Read each statement and check one of the columns to indicate how much you agree or disagree with it.

SA = Strongly Agree   A = Agree   D = Disagree   SD = Strongly Disagree

	SA	A	D	SD
1 Grammar is a set of rules about language use.		✓		
2 Learning grammar means learning how to speak and write effectively in different contexts and situations.		✓		
3 Grammar should be an ongoing focus of attention in L2 teaching.	✓			
4 Grammar needs to be taught as a separate component of the curriculum.			✓	
5 Grammar can best be taught when teaching speaking and writing, that is, when learners are producing language.	✓			
6 Grammar instruction is provided in similar ways across grade levels.				
7 Knowing grammar rules is sufficient for being able to use grammar effectively.				
8 Grammar teaching means correcting students' errors.				
9 Using grammatical terminology is an important part of teaching grammar.				
10 Teachers need to have deep knowledge about grammar in order to teach it.				

Photocopiable © Oxford University Press

Once you have reflected on what *you* think about these statements, ask other teachers what their reactions are. Talk to teachers of different subjects. Ask students of different ages, both native speakers and second language learners. Do they agree? What are the points of greatest disagreement? What do you think the reasons might be for these differences? Why do you think people sometimes have strong feelings about grammar teaching? Write down some notes about what you learn through your conversations with others about grammar teaching, and refer to your notes from time to time as you read the remaining pages of this book. Be on the lookout for new information that may support your current views or raise questions about them. We will return to these statements in Chapter 5.

What Is Grammar?

The word 'grammar' can be used to refer both to what we consciously know about language (grammar 'rules', for example), and to how 'correct' our language is when we are speaking or writing (having 'good grammar' or 'bad grammar'). In this book, we focus on conscious knowledge about language, but we see grammar as more than just a set of rules. We will say more about that below.

Linguists also use the word 'grammar' to refer to the subconscious knowledge about language that we develop as we are born into and grow up in a language community. In that sense, native speakers or early bilinguals develop an understanding of patterns in language that they can rely on to consider whether something 'sounds right' as a means of thinking about what they say. They rely on their internal 'grammar' to tell them how to say what they mean. No one explicitly teaches children the grammar of their mother tongue(s): they just learn it through social interaction and the experiences of communicating in their communities.

Historically, recognizing that children just 'pick up' their mother tongues sometimes led to the view that second language learners, especially children, would also be able to 'pick up' the new language through interaction and experience. In fact, though, as we will see in Chapter 2, many decades of research in L2 classrooms that focus on content through subject-matter instruction—as in French **immersion** programs in Canada—have shown that children in these classrooms do not 'pick up' the language in its full forms. Instead, they often develop ways of speaking and writing that are not faithful to the ways the language needs to be used to be effective in communication, especially in formal and schooling contexts (Harley, Cummins, Swain, & Allen, 1990; Harley & Swain, 1984; Swain, 1985, 1996).

As the research reviewed in Chapter 2 will show, grammar teaching is needed. But teaching grammar does not just mean presenting rules and giving students practice doing exercises that help them follow those rules. Instead, we will see that students need to focus on how language expresses the meanings that it does and to explore the ways those meanings are presented in language as they engage in meaningful tasks. That is the sense in which we will talk about grammar teaching here.

Traditional Grammar Teaching in L1 Contexts

Traditional grammar instruction in **first language (L1)** contexts involves learning rules for correctness and applying them, usually through teaching writing. All students are expected to learn the fine points of the grammar of the standard variety of the languages through which they learn at school. In many contexts around the world, children come to school speaking non-standard varieties of their mother tongues and need to learn the rules of the standard. This means children who do not learn the standard language at home are also language learners at school, and face the added expectation that they will adopt new ways of speaking and writing. Traditional grammar teaching typically focuses on rules for accuracy (for example, in verb forms, plurals, or possessives), rules about verb tense choices, or word order rules. These are important aspects of the language to learn for success in writing and speaking in diverse communicative situations, but it is important that the language children bring to school is also valued and that they are supported in making meaning with the language resources they have developed in their homes and communities (Godley, Sweetland, Wheeler, Minnici, & Carpenter, 2006).

Teachers have found that teaching grammar only as a set of rules, even to native speakers, does not help students learn to be more expressive, creative, or precise in their language choices. In teaching writing, instructors regularly suggest alternative wording when students' phrasing is awkward, propose different organizational strategies when students' texts do not flow easily, and recommend that students think about the audience they are addressing and how their wording choices will be received by that audience. These teachers are drawing students' attention to the language choices that are available to them from the larger 'grammar' of the language, and we see these teachers as also teaching grammar, even if implicitly. Writers choose both form and content, and it is through the rhetorical and syntactic forms they choose that the content is constructed and evaluated. Teachers are intuitively teaching grammar by focusing students' attention on the language alternatives available to them.

In L2 teaching situations, trying to do this work in intuitive ways is challenging, as L2 learners do not have a full range of options in their internal 'grammars' to draw on. So our goal here is to help you talk with your L2 students about the ways the grammatical systems of a language work so that this can be brought to consciousness and the grammar explored in texts of different types. We will also describe activities that engage students in moving from what they know to using new ways of expressing themselves. Below we will present a more developed perspective on how grammar can be infused into L2 teaching in ways that support meaning-making in contexts of schooling, but first we will say a little more about what it means to see grammar as a meaning-making resource.

Grammar and Meaning

Language learning is, at its core, the learning of new ways of making meaning in different situations. L2 learners need to use the new language in ways that enable them to interact with others. In this book, we conceptualize grammar as patterns of language through which meaning is created and shared. This situates grammar teaching in the context of building students' resources for meaning-making by expanding their linguistic repertoires with a focus on form–meaning connections. The ways we use language vary according to the people with whom we are interacting, the subjects about which we are interacting, and our goals in the interaction. That means that expanding students' repertoires for meaning-making in a new language calls for sensitivity to the task, context, and purpose for which they are using the new language. Through grammar instruction, teachers can draw students' attention to the kinds of choices speakers and writers make in accomplishing particular communicative goals.

Grammar enables us to make meaning; we can't make meaning without it. And every language has developed grammatical *systems* through which different kinds of meanings are made. The kinds of systems we're referring to include the mood system that the teacher in Classroom Snapshot 1.1 is exploring with her students. In that system in English, there are three options available to a speaker or writer: declarative, imperative, or interrogative. Other languages have additional mood options, and the grammar of these options is what enables different kinds of meaning-making.

Activity 1.2

Read the following sentences and consider how they differ in their mood options.

1 Did you close the window?
2 Pass me my coat.
3 Everyone feels cold in this room.

Examine the sentences and answer the following questions:

- Where is the verb group?
- What is the subject in each sentence?
- Where in the sentence structure is the subject?
- Can you think of situations in which each sentence would be used? How does each choice of mood contribute to the situation?

The three sentences are in different moods. Sentence 1 is in the interrogative mood; Sentence 2 is in the imperative mood; and Sentence 3 is in the declarative mood. The verb phrases are in bold and the subject is in italics:

1 **Did** *you* **close** the window?
2 **Pass** me my coat.
3 *Everyone* **feels** cold in this room.

Each sentence could be used in the same situation: a group of people are in a cold room and they realize the window should be closed. Each one takes a specific form, but could be understood as a 'command' to close the window. These are different ways to express the same speech function, but the grammar enables the speaker to command in more or less explicit ways.

We saw how the children in Classroom Snapshot 1.1 explored the ways commands, typically presented in imperative mood, can also be presented in declarative or interrogative moods. Let's look at a couple of examples:

- The teacher asks, 'Could you bring me the book from the back of the class?'
- In a writing workshop, the teacher says, 'It might be good to start with a sentence that describes your pet.'

In both of these cases, the student is likely to take what the teacher says as a command. Why do you think this is?

Language is a means of enacting our social lives, and in these examples, the teacher has a relationship of authority that positions the children to see her requests and suggestions as commands, even when the grammatical choices she makes do not take the form of commands. From our perspective in this book, these aspects of language use are also part of grammar teaching. Not all children actually recognize the teacher's requests or suggestions as commands, and they sometimes suffer as a result. (Consider the child whose home and community experiences do not include requests presented as questions, who might answer 'no' when asked if he would like to read the next paragraph!) So teaching grammar means teaching about the different choices available from the systems of the language for making meaning in different contexts.

Other grammatical systems that you will learn about in this book include the systems of *verb meanings*, *logical connection*, and *reference*. In learning about these systems, you and your students discover the different possibilities for meaning that are available to them and that they will encounter in the texts they read and listen to. The focus is on the meanings, but to make the meanings, the forms need to be recognized, learned, and practiced. That is what we mean by grammar teaching.

Variation in Grammar

We just saw how there is variation in the grammatical choices we can make to give a command, depending on the social context we are in and the relationship we have with the persons we are talking to. In addition to variation because of our social roles, language also varies according to what we are doing with it. The language choices we make are good signals of what contexts we are in and what is going on in those contexts. While the vocabulary we use is, of course, often a good clue to what is going on, the grammar we use also plays a role in our understanding of the context of language use.

Activity 1.3

Read the texts below and consider what the context might be. How do the grammatical choices of the speakers and writers help you recognize the situations in which these texts occur?

Text 1

An air mass is a huge body of air that has nearly the same temperature and humidity. Humidity is the amount of water vapor in the air. Air masses form over large areas of land or water. For several days or weeks, an air mass is heated or cooled by the area over which it forms. An air mass that forms in the polar areas will be cool or cold. An air mass that forms in a tropical area will be warm or hot.

(Scott Foresman Science, 2006, p. 190)

Text 2

Speaker 1: What is an air mass?

Speaker 2: It's a mass of air.

Speaker 1: Yes, but what does that mean?

Speaker 2: It's like the text says, it's a body of air.

Text 3

Speaker 1: Do you know what is body of air?

Speaker 2: I think it's like our body.

Speaker 1: Hmm … I don't think so. Maybe it's like, it has its own parts?

Text 4

An air mass is a large body of air. They are important in our world because they are related to our weather. I like air masses because they can be cold or warm.

Each of these texts draws on the same set of vocabulary words, but the grammar helps us see how the words and meanings come from different contexts of use. Text 1 comes from a textbook explanation. You probably recognized this from the ways the definitions are presented, the ways information is densely packed into the clauses and sentences, and the ways the explanation evolves across the text, as words that are introduced are picked up again and defined (as in the case of 'humidity') and concepts are explained (as in the case of 'Air masses form over large areas of land or water').

Text 2 is clearly created in the context of interaction, with one interlocutor pressing the other for a more specific definition. You might suspect that Speaker 1 is a teacher, as the questions asked position Speaker 1 in a more authoritative position vis-à-vis Speaker 2, able to press for further elaboration ('Yes, but what does that mean?').

You may have identified Text 3 as interaction created in pair-work, where both speakers are L2 learners who are exploring meaning in a text they are reading.

Text 4 could be a spoken presentation or a written report by a student. We recognize this as student work from the overall structure, with its comment at the end about liking air masses, something we might not find appropriate for this kind of text.

As these examples show, the language we use signals that the context may be formal or informal; that we are interacting with others to co-construct meaning; that we are speaking or writing. Even when the topic and subject area are the same, the language is infinitely variable in the meanings it can make, drawing from the potential of the grammar in different ways as we do different things in different contexts.

Our focus in this book is mainly on contexts of schooling and the grammatical forms students will encounter in the language used in learning. This language, sometimes called **academic language**, has been defined as 'the ability to understand and express, in both oral and written modes, concepts and ideas that are relevant to success in school'(Cummins & Man, 2007, p. 797). The language that students encounter at school is different from the language they use in informal ways in their everyday lives. Academic language involves learning not just new vocabulary but also whole new ways of structuring sentences and texts, interacting with a reader, and presenting a point of view. This can be very challenging. In this book, you will learn ways to teach grammar that help students recognize and engage with the meanings made in the kinds of texts they will encounter in learning school subjects. This will help them develop L2 proficiency in service of success in learning.

We can only learn a new language when we are able to put it to meaningful and purposeful use. We need to have a reason to find new ways of making meaning and to have successful experiences that support us in continuing to do so. Children are generally motivated to succeed in school, and you can support their success through methods of teaching grammar that contribute to their learning of academic language. But to learn academic language, children need teachers who can help them understand how language works in the texts they encounter. They need experience engaging with academic language in meaningful contexts of speaking, listening, reading, and writing activities, guided by teachers who can focus them on structures in the language and explain what they mean.

Even in stories that seem to be about everyday life, the language used to construct the plot, characters, and themes is quite different from the 'everyday' language that constructs interactions in our daily lives. And even in the early grades, the language that presents the school curriculum is often literary or scientific, drawing on words and structures that children rarely encounter outside of school. A common response to this difficulty is to provide struggling learners with 'easier' material, simplifying the curriculum. While simplified texts have a role to play in learning, it is also important to expand students' engagement with grade-level texts and support learners in accessing meaning in texts that might appear to be 'too hard'. Children can learn to recognize patterns of language in the texts they read and use those patterns in their own speaking and writing. This book will illustrate some ways of drawing their attention to, supporting their engagement with, and promoting their use of those patterns.

Differences in expectations for academic language use emerge as teachers and children move from one disciplinary context to another, as each subject area has its expected activities and ways of using language to accomplish them. For example, the language that students need to discuss a story they have read is different from the language that they will use in working together to do a science experiment. Writing a book report in Language Arts calls for different ways of using language than writing a report of a science experiment. In both oral and written academic tasks, language resources are used in a variety of ways according to the purpose at hand. The teacher who understands the ways grammatical choices shift as children move from one context to another can provide specific learning opportunities that prepare children to engage successfully in classroom activities across content areas, developing language and content knowledge simultaneously.

Who Needs to Learn Grammar?

The students we have in mind in this book are in primary and secondary school classrooms in various contexts of second language learning, and so we address the teaching of grammar by focusing on the kinds of tasks and texts that students typically engage with across the years of schooling. The goal of this book is to show how research supports the teaching of grammar in meaningful ways in classroom learning. In Chapter 2, we will read about the role of grammar instruction in supporting the attention-focusing and **noticing** that research shows is so important for learning language in school settings.

There are different reasons children are learning a second or foreign language, and different situations in which they are taught. Across these contexts, we often see a variety of approaches to grammar teaching. Second language (L2) learners are quite diverse, as they come from different linguistic and cultural backgrounds, have varying levels of proficiency, and differ in the knowledge of school subjects they have developed in their first languages. But regardless of their backgrounds, they are expected to study school subjects across numerous disciplines. These students also need to engage with a lot of variation in the language as they encounter it in oral and written forms, in formal and informal contexts, and in a range of subject areas. That makes second language learning in school very challenging. Learning to read, write, and interact using academic language requires support for language development that assists students in meeting the communicative and **literacy** demands of disciplinary learning.

Many language learners who are learning an L2 in a second language context—for example, as members of an immigrant community—continue to struggle with academic language and academic subjects even after several years in the new language environment. Newly arrived immigrants with little or no proficiency in the L2 need intensive support for language development and this is often provided in classrooms specially dedicated to their instruction. In many cases, however, students who are still developing proficiency in the language of instruction are placed directly in mainstream classrooms for most subject-area learning, and much of their language learning takes place without continued support from language specialists.

In the approach to L2 grammar teaching that we present in this book, we are envisioning students and teachers in a range of language learning contexts. The activities and approaches we present are designed to help you focus on grammar with students at all levels of L2 proficiency. Even advanced learners need ongoing attention to the ways language works in the texts they read and write, and in support of their speaking and listening. The following are examples of some of the contexts in which the approach presented here can apply:

Learners in Immigrant Communities

Children vary greatly in their experiences with language outside of school, making it especially important that academic language **registers** become a focus of attention in the classroom. The increasing number of language-minority children in today's classrooms has stimulated much research on academic language, but language-minority students are themselves a diverse group. In the US context, some of these students are **English language learners** (**ELLs**), still in the process of learning the language across registers and modalities, while others are fluent speakers of English from communities where English does not serve as the language of familial or community communication, and where, for various reasons, the range of registers they are able to develop does not include those that are expected at school. English language learners also vary in the extent to which they have had the opportunity to engage in a range of registers in their home languages. For example, older children who immigrate to the United States, having learned literacy and had the experience of using academic language in their home country's education system, may be well positioned to learn academic English because the notion of 'schooled' ways of speaking and writing will already be familiar. On the other hand, ELLs who have few opportunities to participate in activities that draw on English academic registers outside of school may need substantial support to develop them (as will many native speakers of English who do not have exposure to these registers outside of school).

Many ESL learners are in mainstream primary or secondary classrooms, where they need attention to language in ways that can also support the learning of all students. Gibbons (2006b) offered three principles for curriculum planning in such contexts: use of authentic curriculum materials, assignment of tasks that are intellectually and cognitively challenging, and provision of support through scaffolding. She urged that teachers analyze the language demands of each topic, select focus language on this basis, and design activities to teach the focus language. She illustrated how this is done by looking first at the larger context: moving from the text to specific language features, from meaning in context to language form, and from what is known to what is new.

Learners in Content-Based Language Teaching (CBLT) Classrooms

In content-based language teaching classrooms, students are learning in a language that is new to them (Lightbown, 2014). Immersion programs teach school subjects through the medium of a second language to students who typically share the same L1, so an ongoing challenge is to support their use of the L2 in a range of contexts, both formal and informal (Lyster, 2007). As children in immersion programs usually continue to learn the L2 throughout the years of schooling, their teachers need ways of understanding developments in the grammar that can be supported across the school years. Dual immersion programs, also called two-way immersion, teach literacy and academic content in two languages, with balanced numbers of native-speaking students of each language integrated for instruction. Literacy and content instruction is provided to both groups in the two languages.

Sheltered instruction is a content-based approach to teaching second language learners that provides instruction in the content areas while they are still in the early stages of L2 learning. It emphasizes specific support for language learners to be able to access the content area curriculum in the language they are learning (Lightbown, 2014). Though these classrooms may be more common in a second language context, where students are learning both a new language and new subjects, CBLT can also occur in foreign language classrooms. Cummins and Man (2007) describe this kind of classroom, where students are learning in English with a **communicative** task-based syllabus, at a secondary school in Hong Kong. They suggest that in such contexts there is a need for subject-matter teachers to see themselves as language teachers and direct students' attention to **lexical**, grammatical, and discourse features of the language. If instead teachers choose to use simplified texts, students may not have opportunities to grapple with the theories, issues, and concerns of the subject matter at an appropriate academic level for secondary students. A focus on grammar can provide such students with the more demanding instruction they need. **Content and Language Integrated Learning (CLIL)** is an approach to content-based language teaching developed primarily in Europe to expand L2 learning opportunities for students in secondary school classrooms. CLIL classroom teachers approach the language of the subject matter from the point of view of its role in understanding and learning the discipline, seeing language and content as inseparable (Llinares, Morton, & Whittaker, 2012).

Learners in Foreign Language Programs

Foreign language programs offer instruction in a language that is not typically spoken in the students' out-of-school context. They aim to develop learners' proficiency in a language they may use in the future. The greatest challenge in foreign language teaching is providing robust opportunities for children to use the language in meaningful ways. Introducing some content-based instruction is one way of providing such opportunities.

How Does Grammar Teaching Fit into the L2 Classroom?

The needs of L2 students are different from those of L1 students when it comes to grammar instruction, as L2 students need more information about form–meaning connections than do native speakers of a language. As discussed above, L2 learners do not have the same intuitions about the target language, so asking them to think about 'what sounds right' is not going to be effective. Instead, L2 learners need to have their attention drawn to the ways grammar is used in the texts they read, and when they write, they need to be encouraged to draw on the grammar they have been taught. In addition, they need opportunities to talk about language form and meaning connections. According to Ellis (2006):

> *Grammar teaching* involves any instructional technique that draws learners' attention to some specific grammatical form in such a way that it helps them either to understand it metalinguistically and/or process it in comprehension and/or production so that they can internalize it.
>
> (Ellis, 2006, p. 84)

In Chapter 2, you will read about the theories we draw on to support the approach to grammar presented here. Sociocultural theories help us recognize that language is learned through meaningful interaction in contexts of use, and have informed current theories of second language development. The theories of second language development, however, also highlight the need to raise learners' awareness of language by building explicit attention to language into the meaningful interactions in which we engage young learners. Complementing those theoretical perspectives, functional linguistics theory provides us with a useful metalanguage for making explicit form–meaning connections in meaningful contexts of language use that also support students' learning of school subjects.

Form-focused instruction in L2 grammar can be **planned** or **incidental** (Ellis, 2001, 2006). *Planned* grammar instruction means being proactive in selecting features for focus, while *incidental* focus on form occurs spontaneously within communicative activities, when teachers provide feedback to students on their language use. An important aim of this book is to demonstrate how you can develop form-focused instruction across a unit of study, including planned attention to meaning as well as form, and then incorporate incidental attention to form through learning activities involving different types of language use.

In this book, we make the case for providing feedback that will focus first on meaning rather than form. This may be different from what you think of as your responsibility in teaching grammar, which has traditionally emphasized helping students to be more accurate in their use of target language structures. For example, in a recent classroom observation study in four English as a second language (ESL) and four French as a second language (FSL) high school classrooms, Simard & Jean (2011) observed that teachers consistently drew learners' attention to form separately from meaning-based practice. In fact, their study identified almost no discourse-level discussion or text-oriented talk about language.

Yet the point of learning grammar is to be able to participate in discourse, so any approach to grammar instruction needs to support students not just in being correct in surface form at the word level but also in drawing on language structures that enable them to participate meaningfully. This is important in L2 classrooms where language is the focus of instruction as well as in L2 classrooms where students are learning a language through subject-matter instruction. For this purpose, going beyond feedback on **morphological** forms and grammatical structures is necessary. Teachers need to be proactive in helping students recognize the resources available to them in the language and use them in spoken and written discourse. That means grammar instruction needs to be planned so that students' attention is drawn to the ways their linguistic choices may present different kinds of meanings, highlighting the resources they can exploit when they speak and write to be effective in their classroom learning.

As you read this book, it will be evident that the approach to grammar instruction presented here does not view grammar as something to be taught separately from content. Instead, we show how L2 grammar teaching can be fully integrated into instruction addressing the goals and curriculum that the teacher is working with. As you will read in Chapter 2, a focus on language form is best situated in meaningful contexts of language use. For teachers and students, the most meaningful contexts of language use are the instructional activities they are engaged in for learning content. You will learn how to situate talk about the language in the exploration of the texts your students are reading, need to draw on in talk and writing, and that are useful for classroom activities. Teaching grammar in this way means you focus on what is to be learned and identify the language demands of that learning. Those language demands help you decide what grammar to teach. The texts and activities use that language to present curriculum content. They then provide meaningful contexts in which to focus on grammar, as the activities also give students the practice and experience they need to develop confidence and expertise in using the grammatical forms.

You will see that the approach to grammar presented in Chapters 3 and 4 begins by identifying the curricular goals that you have for a particular instructional unit. We take the *unit of instruction* as the context for deciding what grammar to teach, not individual lessons. Students' learning needs to extend over multiple opportunities to engage with the language and grammar to be learned in different modes, that is, through:

- teacher explanation
- talk between teacher and students and between students themselves
- exploration of written texts
- speaking or writing assignments in which students present what they have learned using the grammar in focus, and can be assessed on their learning of grammar as well as content.

Below we provide two examples of how a focus on grammar can be infused into a unit of content instruction. Of course, there cannot be a single way of moving through a unit of instruction across all subjects, but we can see how this approach might work in an elementary classroom and a secondary history classroom. We describe four steps that can be taken to assign a central role to grammar teaching in different ways; how these steps are realized in lessons will depend on your context and goals. These are examples of *macro scaffolding* by planning challenging work with language and content (Schleppegrell & O'Hallaron, 2011). In Chapter 2, we will describe *micro scaffolding* moves that can be incorporated throughout a unit of instruction as teachers and students interact about language and meaning.

Infusing a Focus on Grammar into an Instructional Unit at the Primary Level: An Example from Language Arts

Refer to Classroom Snapshot 1.1 (see page 4), where ELL students in a Grade 2 Language Arts classroom are reading the story *Officer Buckle and Gloria*. The book is about a police officer who visits elementary schools and gives lectures on safety.

Step 1: Setting goals, motivating the learning, and engaging with a 'text'

The teacher is introducing a story that the class will work with over the next week or two. As the teacher introduces the text, she also introduces some language for talking about the language of the text in meaningful ways. For example, she might suggest that in reading, talking, and writing about the story over the next week, the class will focus on how the author uses 'commands' in the story. The class can identify some commands and talk about when and why someone gives a command. The focus at this point, though, is engaging children in talk about the story, drawing on their background knowledge and motivating their interest. The class engages in a read-aloud activity that introduces them to the story.

Step 2: Exploring the language of the text, using metalanguage, to put the forms in focus in meaningful context

After the students have read the story for enjoyment and understanding, the teacher leads them in activities where they focus in on the ways the author has presented commands in the story, as these are central to the plot and to understanding the characters. They unpack the written language, looking at how commands are formed, the kinds of commands that are in the story, and the different ways commands are written, using the metalanguage of *declarative*, *interrogative*, and *imperative*, along with *command*, *question*, *statement*, and *offer*. This is the point in the lesson where the kind of activity illustrated in Classroom Snapshot 1.1 takes place.

Step 3: Maintaining a focus on the grammar to be learned, continuing to draw students' attention to the language as it is encountered

Now that the students have had an opportunity to reflect on the forms, use, and meanings of commands, the teacher keeps a focus on commands throughout the remainder of the unit of instruction. She will be alert to the children's use of commands and will draw attention to them, restating what the children say and highlighting the use of language relevant to understanding and using commands. Students will be given opportunities to work together to identify commands in other kinds of relevant texts and will help each other remember how commands are given in different ways.

Step 4: Engaging students in using the language in meaningful ways that call for use of the grammar in focus

When the teacher sees that the children are using commands and the language they have learned for talking about commands, she sets spoken or written assignments that call for their use. For example, after reading the story, the children could be asked to write a set of 'safety tips' for the classroom using the grammar of commands.

In the secondary school, the learning goals are driven by the content to be learned in more focused ways than in the primary school, where divisions between subject areas are less pronounced. That means that in the secondary school it is crucial that grammar be taught in the service of the content learning, and that the teacher consider the content goals in identifying the relevant language features.

Infusing a Focus on Grammar into an Instructional Unit at the Secondary Level: An Example from History

Step 1: Setting goals, motivating the learning, and engaging with a 'text'

The history teacher is beginning a unit of study on the debates over slavery in the USA in the nineteenth century. He will be using texts from a number of sources to introduce students to the different points of view and perspectives presented in debates in Congress and the press. In reviewing those texts, he recognizes that key language features that students will encounter in those texts are the *saying* and *thinking* processes of the historical figures who participated in the debates. He also knows that the students will need to be able to compare and contrast those points of view in an essay they will write at the end of the unit.

With this goal in mind, the teacher tells the class that as they learn about the debates over slavery, they will focus on how authors represent the saying and thinking of the historical figures, and think about the language they will need to use to contrast the different points of view.

Step 2: Exploring the language of the text, using metalanguage, to put the forms in focus in meaningful context

After developing some background knowledge about the debates, the students read speeches and articles that presented different points of view on the issue at that time. The teacher also brings examples of texts that discuss those points of view. He works with the class to **deconstruct** some examples of the ways authors write about the different perspectives that were taken. As a class and then in small groups and pairs, the teacher and students explore the written texts, looking at how the authors use verbs of saying and thinking to present different perspectives, and focusing on the meanings contributed by the **conjunctions** and **connectors** that contrast different points of view with each other. The teacher introduces and develops the metalanguage of *saying* and *thinking/feeling processes*, and *conjunctions of comparison and contrast.*

Step 3: Maintaining a focus on the grammar to be learned, continuing to draw students' attention to the language as it is encountered

Now that the students have looked at the ways authors present historical debates and contrast different perspectives, the teacher keeps a focus on these language features throughout the remainder of the unit of instruction. He is alert to students talking about the points of view and draws attention to the ways they position different perspectives, restating what the students say and highlighting the use of language relevant to presenting and contrasting views. He models sentences in which speech or thought is reported and quoted, and gives students practice in quoting and reporting points of view. Students are given opportunities to work together to report on and contrast the views of the different historical figures.

Step 4: Engaging students in using the language in meaningful ways that call for use of the grammar in focus

When the teacher sees that the students are able to use language they have learned for talking about different points of view, he introduces the writing assignment that calls for them to use this language. He provides examples of how the essays they will write can be organized and structured. He also highlights the expectation that they will quote or report on the saying and thinking of different historical figures, and that they will engage in comparison and contrast using the conjunctions and connectors they have focused on in their reading. In evaluating their essays, he comments both on the meaning they have developed and on the forms the language takes in reporting, quoting, and contrasting views.

In these examples, we see how grammar teaching can be planned and carried out through a series of steps that keep the language and content goals in focus:

- The teacher identifies the larger goals for the unit of instruction, aligned with the content expectations of the curriculum, and selects a grammar focus that will support the content learning.
- The learners' attention is drawn to the meanings and functions that the focus on grammar will support.
- The class talks about the grammar (its form and what it means), using grammatical metalanguage to identify and notice the forms, and deconstructs written texts to see how the grammar works in meaningful contexts of use.
- The teacher guides children to pay attention to the grammar in focus as they speak and write throughout the unit of instruction.
- The children complete a task that engages them in meaningful work in which the grammar is useful to them. Their performance in this work offers the teacher an opportunity to assess their learning.

Through this process of selecting grammar from meaningful texts, talking about the grammar (its form and what it means), analyzing the grammar in written texts, focusing learners' attention on the grammar when they speak, and engaging the learners in meaningful work in which the grammar is useful to them, you will help them develop language resources relevant to the work they are doing.

Teaching and Learning Functional Grammar

A focus on meaning draws attention to the contexts in which language is used. Recognizing that their language choices are influenced by the situations in which they are participating helps students become more flexible in their language use. One of the key points of this book is to show how the grammar we use depends on what it is we are doing with language and who we are interacting with. The subject area, task, and context all influence the language we use. In schools, the situational variation includes differences in the way language is used across subjects. These subject-area demands can help language teachers think about the grammar that needs to be taught and use grammar teaching as a means of accomplishing their content goals.

A focus on meaning in context also implies that the main purpose of grammar teaching may not be to promote accuracy in language use. Errors are a natural part of second language development, so L2 learners have to make errors in order to grow in language proficiency. That means our primary objective in teaching grammar should be that of expanding learners' resources for meaning-making by addressing both form and meaning. L2 learners bring varied grammatical resources to school, and it is in classroom contexts that L2 learners will further develop those resources and learn new ways of using language.

For these reasons, we take a functional grammar approach in this book. Developed by linguist Michael Halliday (1978, 1994), functional grammar offers tools for seeing how meaning is constructed in language. It helps us recognize that words come in patterns, and that students can learn to see the meaning in those patterns. Halliday (2004) reminds us that in schooling, students have to learn *language*, learn *through* language, and learn *about* language, and he points out that learning *about* language is often neglected. **Functional grammar instruction** has been widely adopted in Australia and adapted and implemented in many parts of the world, including Europe, Asia, Latin America, and North America. In a functional grammar approach, the teacher begins with a focus on meaning and helps students recognize the forms that work together to make that meaning. Both vocabulary and what we traditionally think of as 'grammar' are involved in this meaning-making, so often the grammar teaching we describe will also promote examination of the forms and meanings of words.

This book shows how you can put a focus on language in content teaching to enable all students to be successful with the language through which schooling is accomplished. One method of achieving this is to engage students in discussion about language, raising their awareness of the way knowledge is constructed in language in different subjects. Language itself, while clearly the means through which learning is construed and evaluated, is a neglected area of discussion in many classrooms. Teachers can engage students in analyzing the ways language is powerful in constructing knowledge so that they can also participate in that construction. This approach fits well into contexts where teachers are teaching language through content-based approaches.

All of the activities in this book are designed to help you nurture a reflective attitude on the part of students and help them recognize how language choices create meanings of different kinds. The activities provide guidance in talking with children about text to deconstruct explanations, in looking at how concepts are presented and developed, and in equipping students to learn from other texts. Functional grammar activities give children opportunities to think deeply about the texts they read, and work with the language in the texts to develop greater confidence in recognizing what it means and using it themselves. Students may resist rereading a text just for the sake of reading it again, but the functional grammar activities will help them read and reread the texts in your curriculum with a purpose, maintaining their interest as they find new meaning in the text and explore the language. The activities also give students opportunities to rehearse new ways of using language orally, before writing. And finally, functional grammar activities prepare children to write more effectively, using their newly developed understandings about language to explore novel ways of communicating their own meanings.

We will have much more to say about functional approaches to grammar teaching in the remaining chapters of this book, emphasizing the following points:

- Functional grammar draws students' attention to language forms and how different language forms make different kinds of meaning, connecting with curriculum contexts. This means students are learning the grammar they need to succeed in the reading, speaking, and writing tasks they are asked to do.
- Functional grammar seeks to expand students' linguistic repertoires.
- Functional grammar learning is motivating because students are focusing on the language they need for learning, not on decontextualized exercises.
- Functional grammar supports academic language development because it emphasizes the language of the curriculum and draws students' attention to the ways language is used in school subjects.
- Functional grammar instruction is efficient because the language taught is the language that students need to work with in their present tasks.

What Do Teachers Need to Know to Teach Grammar?

Teachers at all levels and in all L2 learning contexts need to be supported in providing opportunities for continuing language development for their students, even for those who may speak the second language with colloquial fluency. Such students often still have much to learn about language to develop the reading, writing, and academic language they need for full participation and success in academic subject areas. In a review of research on language learning in the secondary school, Schleppegrell and O'Halloran (2011) suggest that secondary teachers of L2 learners also need knowledge about the language demands of different content areas to support the learning of academic language across all subjects. Teachers need to be able to plan challenging work that helps students develop language and content knowledge over time and involves students in learning, and they need to support students' engagement with language and content in the moment-to-moment instruction in the classroom. Other researchers also call for new ways of helping teachers and teacher educators explore the linguistic features of academic **genres** and provide **explicit instruction** about language beyond understanding vocabulary (for example, Janzen, 2007). Functional grammar is a means of doing just that. Gebhard, Chen, Graham, and Gunawan (2013), for example, describe how students in a TESOL master's degree program used functional grammar to design curriculum and instruction. In doing so, their ways of thinking about grammar 'shifted from a traditional sentence-level, form-focused perspective to a more functional understanding' (p. 107).

You may wonder what kind of technical language this book assumes of the reader. We do expect that you will be familiar with traditional grammatical terminology such as *noun, verb, conjunction,* and *clause*. If you need to brush up on these terms, there are many resources available to you (see Suggestions for Further Reading on page 123). When we introduce other terminology, we will explain it. We have found that a teacher can get started with infusing grammar instruction into teaching even with only a little understanding of grammar, and that by engaging children in activities that promote noticing of language, the teacher comes to greater understanding.

As you work through this book, you will learn to make a focus on language engaging. We will help you and your students develop a common language for talking about how language works.

Summary

In this chapter, you have been invited to reflect on what you already know about grammar teaching and how you think it can work in practice. We have described some of the contexts in which children learn grammar in the primary and secondary classroom, and have presented the role teachers play in grammar instruction. In Chapter 2, we will highlight theory and research that informs the ways grammar is taught to L2 learners.

2
Teaching and Learning Grammar

Preview

This chapter reviews the theories that help us understand how grammar is best learned and how classroom teaching can support grammar learning. The theoretical perspectives most important for this understanding include sociocultural orientations to teaching and learning; perspectives on language development that see it emerging in contexts of meaningful interaction including explicit focus on form and meaning; and a functional theory of language in use. As we will see, theory that helps explain how language is learned has informed research on grammar teaching in K-12 classrooms, and that research has further contributed to our ideas about how best to infuse grammar teaching into classroom instruction.

Social, Cognitive, and Functional Perspectives

The key feature of the approach to grammar teaching presented in this book is that it is situated in authentic contexts of language use and is discourse-based. This approach builds from Vygotsky's sociocultural perspective on learning (for example, Vygotsky, 1978, 1986). From that perspective, we understand that cognitive activity and social activity are not separate; learning takes place in and results from the specific interactions we have in particular settings. Participating in interaction provides opportunities for language use, and that participation enables learners to internalize new ways of using language. In other words, what we experience in social interaction shapes our knowledge about language and about the world. In this book, the social contexts we focus on are classrooms, where we show how best to support learning of the language needed to engage with school subjects and interact in contexts of schooling. Vygotsky also suggests that teachers, as more knowledgeable users of the language, can offer students opportunities to engage with learning at levels slightly beyond their current abilities, supporting them in noticing and using language in new ways and guiding them in language production through speaking or writing.

Recent theories of second language development have drawn on sociocultural theory to propose a view of language learning that suggests an orientation to both form and meaning (Lightbown & Spada, 2013). Research consistently supports the view that attention to language needs to be in the context of meaningful activity (Ellis, Basturkman, & Loewen, 2002). From this perspective, second languages are developed through interaction where students have frequent encounters with the language to be learned in meaningful contexts of use, and where attention to form and meaning is explicitly promoted. Second language development is not a smooth pathway. Learners do not begin producing language accurately simply because they know grammatical rules and are given feedback on form. They may continue making errors and using forms infelicitously as they speak and write, and they need many encounters with the language to be learned.

A new language is not learned by picking up one bit at a time until it is learned once and for all, but instead emerges through encounters with the new language and opportunities to use it and focus on it (Ellis & Larsen-Freeman, 2006). Ellis and Larsen-Freeman point out that the terms used to describe the mechanisms for **second language acquisition (SLA)** are all mental actions: 'noticing, selective attending, noticing the gap, ... ' (p. 569). But they also point out that '[l]anguage use, social roles, language learning, and conscious experience are all socially situated, negotiated, scaffolded, and guided' (p. 572). Language learning involves social and cognitive processes, and classroom learning offers a context where both aspects can be fostered. We will see that research supports the notion that explicit attention to language form, particularly for learners in communicative and content-based instructional settings, is necessary to enable the levels of language development needed for success in school. Grammar teaching promotes the *noticing* and *awareness raising* that is necessary for second language development in contexts of schooling.

The sociocultural perspective is also supported by Michael Halliday's (1978, 1994) theory of language that provides the functional grammar perspective presented in this book. According to this theory, language is a meaning-making resource that offers us systems of meanings through which we enact our social lives and construe our experiences of the world. The theory offers a meaningful metalanguage, language that enables us to link form and meaning in ways that facilitate children's learning of second and foreign languages in school settings. We will discuss the importance of grammatical metalanguage in being explicit about how language works, and show how metalanguage enables the noticing and focus necessary for language development. We will see how grammar can be addressed through talk about text that focuses on language choices, and how classroom talk about grammar can support students' reading, speaking, writing, and content learning.

We offer an overview of the key aspects of this theory that inform our thinking about grammar teaching and learning. We also introduce a pedagogical framework based in the theory that will guide our presentation of approaches to grammar teaching in Chapters 3 and 4. This framework, based on the research of Pauline Gibbons (2006a), draws on sociocultural theory and Halliday's theory of language to offer a set of moves teachers can make in support of learning grammar in contexts of authentic language use in classrooms.

Interaction and Language Learning

Although the notion that learners only needed **comprehensible input** for language development has been popular for some time (Krashen, 1982), it has now become clear that learners also need focused attention on language itself to attain high levels of accuracy and control over a new language. Evidence from Canadian French immersion education, for example, has shown that just participating in naturalistic learning in the classroom does not lead to high levels of grammatical competence (Genesee, 1987; Harley et al., 1990; Harley & Swain, 1984; Swain, 1985, 1996). Swain (1996) found that when grammar was taught in immersion classrooms, it was often done in isolation from meaningful contexts of language use. This led to significant shortcomings in the development of learners' language. Immersion students often attained some fluency in the target language, along with high levels of comprehension ability in listening and reading, but continued to experience problems with grammatical accuracy in their oral and written production. In her observations of immersion classes, Swain (1996) noted that some forms of the language to be learned rarely occurred in the language directed to students (certain verb tenses, for example), providing no opportunity for those forms to be learned through comprehensible input, much less focused on or practiced. She suggested that teachers needed to plan for teaching that would provide students with opportunities to notice and focus on language forms in meaningful contexts of use.

Swain drew on sociocultural theory to argue that it is the meaningful use of the new language that promotes its full development. In an influential article supported by extensive research in Canadian French immersion programs, Swain (1985) proposed that **comprehensible output** is needed to move learners toward greater proficiency. She has continued to argue that language production is itself a source of learning, and that learners need to be prompted to use alternative forms to express themselves more accurately or precisely (Swain, 1995). Swain and Lapkin (2002) further suggested that through talk, the language being learned can be made an object of analysis, and that this is valuable in focusing students' attention and enabling L2 learning. Language production is not just *evidence* of language development in this view. Instead, it actively *supports* that development as it enhances fluency through practice, promotes noticing to trigger new linguistic knowledge and hypothesis-testing, and enables learners to 'control and internalize linguistic knowledge' (Swain, 1995, p. 126). In other words, the need to produce language promotes learning language.

Both teacher–student and student–student interaction offer social contexts where learners can focus on and reflect on language forms and meanings. Swain and Lapkin (2002) show the value of student–student interaction about language. They report on a study that engaged Grade 7 (12-year-old) French immersion students in dialogue as they wrote, and then again as they discussed corrections to their writing and rewrote. The researchers found that having the students speak with each other stimulated debate about the meanings being made and the forms to use. Swain and Lapkin refer to this as '**metatalk**', and suggest that conscious reflection on language use through metatalk 'is one sort of collaborative dialogue—dialogue in which speakers are engaged in problem-solving and knowledge-building' (p. 286). Collaborative talk about language, as we will see in Chapters 3 and 4, is a means for learners to focus on form and meaning in authentic contexts of language use.

Classroom Snapshot 2.1

Swain (1995) reports on how Keith and George, 13-year-old Grade 8 French immersion students, reconstruct a dictated text in an activity called *dictogloss* (Wajnryb, 1990). They were focusing on both content and grammar, and had done this kind of activity several times already. Here, they are reconstructing the first sentence of the dictogloss:

En ce qui concerne l'environnement, il y a beaucoup de problèmes qui nous tracassent. [As far as the environment is concerned, there are many problems which worry us.] (p. 133)

In this segment, the two students are negotiating their understanding of the form and meaning of *tracassent*. They have looked up the verb *tracasser* in a reference book, and have realized that *nous* cannot be the subject of the clause, as the verb does not have the ending it would have in that case. Here, Keith asks the teacher about this, and she focuses the students on the actual subject of the clause, *problèmes*, deliberately not providing the answer to his question:

1 **Keith:**   (…) *'Tracasse', 'aimons', n'est-ce pas que 'tracasse'* [to teacher who has just arrived], *ce n'est pas 'nous tracasse'* [what he has written down in his notes], *c'est 'nous tracassons'?* [*Tracasse, aimons,* isn't it *tracasse,* it's not *nous tracasse,* it's *nous tracassons?*]

2 **Teacher:**   *Ce sont des PROBLÈMES qui nous tracassent.* [It's the *problems* that are worrying us.]

      (…)

3 **George:**   Oh! [beginning to realize what is happening]

      (…)

      Les problèmes qui nous tracassent. Like the … *c'est les problèmes* … like, that concerns us.

      (…)

      'Tracasse' c'est pas un, c'est pas un … [*Tracasse,* it's not a, it's not a …] *Oui,* I dunno [unable to articulate what he has discovered].

4 **Keith:**   *OK, ça dit 'les problèmes qui nous tracassent'. Donc, est-ce que 'tracasse' est un verbe? Qu'on, qu'on doit conjuguer?* [OK, it says 'the problems which worry us'. Therefore, is *tracasse* a verb? That you, that you have to conjugate?]

5 **Teacher:**   Uh huh.

6 **Keith:**   *Donc est-ce que c'est 'tracassons'?* [So is it *tracassons?*]

7 **Teacher:**   *Ce sont les PROBLÈMES qui nous tracassent.* [It's the *problems* which are worrying us.]

      (…)

8 **George:**   *Nous, c'est, c'est pas, c'est pas, oui, c'est les problèmes, c'est pas, c'est pas 'nous'.* [Us, it's, it's not, it's not, yeah, it's the problems, it's not, it's not *us.*]

9 **Keith:**   *Ah! E-n-t* [in French] *OK, OK.*

(Swain, 1995, pp. 133–4)

Keith knows that *nous tracasse* does not fit with what he knows about French: that the verb ending is *–ons* when *nous* is the subject. The students cannot find the form in the book they consult. When they ask the teacher, she hints by stressing *problèmes*, but does not give them the answer. Finally, at 3, George begins to grasp the way the words are related to each other and the students work out the answer. We see how George and Keith together realize that *nous* is not the subject of the verb *tracassent*; *les problèmes*, represented by *qui*, is the subject. As Swain points out, this realization calls for understanding the *meaning* of the sentence. She observes that the students are able to be explicit about the basis for their insight and connect form, function, and meaning, even without much grammatical metalanguage. ■

Along with language use and grammar teaching situated in authentic social contexts of interaction, learners need multiple opportunities to focus on language and meaning and *notice* language form. Interacting with others to discuss language forms and meaning helps learners come to understand how the grammar of the language works in contexts of use and how grammatical choices shape the meanings that are made. In this book, you will see many examples of focus on form in classroom interaction that supports language learning as students engage with school subjects.

Noticing and Awareness-Raising

Noticing means paying attention to the linguistic features of the language to be learned (Nassaji & Fotos, 2004; Schmidt, 1990). Many researchers have confirmed that drawing learners' attention to form–meaning connections plays an important role in moving them toward advanced levels of language use. For some researchers (for example, Swain, 1995), noticing has been seen as a means of helping learners identify a gap between what they want to say and what they are able to say. We will be expanding that view of the role of noticing to show how noticing also promotes learners' consciousness about the choices they can make when engaged in meaning-making tasks.

Grammar teaching is sometimes prompted by learner errors, as teachers respond by providing feedback on grammatical accuracy. While this book goes beyond a reactive focus on form in grammar teaching, it is valuable to consider what researchers have learned in conducting research on feedback. Lyster and Ranta (1997), for example, studied the ways teachers go about helping students notice their errors and focus on the correct forms. They identified six types of feedback that teachers provided to students in communicative interaction in four French immersion classrooms at the primary level. Teachers responded to students' phonological, lexical, and grammatical errors through explicit correction, **recast**, clarification requests, metalinguistic clues, elicitation, and repetition.

Activity 2.1

The following are definitions of the six types of feedback Lyster and Ranta describe. Can you match the teacher response with the type of feedback it illustrates?

Type of feedback	Definition from Lyster and Ranta (1997)
Explicit correction	Teacher provides the correct form or clearly indicates that what was said was incorrect.
Recasts	Teacher reformulates what was said, minus the error.
Clarification requests	Teacher indicates that the utterance has been misunderstood or is ill-formed in some way and requires repetition or reformulation.
Metalinguistic feedback	Teacher indicates that there is an error without providing the correct form.
Elicitation	Teacher asks students to reformulate their utterance or uses a question to elicit the correct form, or asks the student to complete an utterance.
Repetition	Teacher repeats the student's error, often with intonation that highlights the error.

Table 2.1 Definitions of types of feedback (from Lyster & Ranta, 1997)

Student–teacher interaction	Type of feedback
1 **St:** Hmm … the childs. The nice childs are here. **T:** Can we say 'the childs'?	*EC*
2 **St:** We cutted the straws into six pieces. **T:** We say 'we cut the straws into six pieces', even though it's past tense. 'Cut' is an irregular verb.	*EC* *MF – explained error*
3 **St:** May, May I writes a letter … for my sister? **T:** Excuse me?	*CE*
4 **St:** The cat can runs. **T:** The cat can runs? The cat can …	*E*
5 **St:** The childs. **T:** The childs?	*Repetition*
6 **St:** Mary made the cake by her. **T:** Oh. Mary made the cake by herself.	*Recast*

Photocopiable © Oxford University Press

Table 2.2 Examples of types of feedback

The first student–teacher interaction is an example of *metalinguistic feedback*. The student should have said 'the children'. The teacher in this case is indicating to the student that there is an error without providing the correct form, by asking 'Can we say "the childs"?' The teacher in the second interaction provides *explicit correction*. The student uses the incorrect form of the verb 'cut'. The teacher tells the student explicitly what the correct form is, and that 'cut' is irregular. The third student–teacher exchange is an example of a *clarification request*, as the teacher responds to the student with 'Excuse me?'. Exchange four is an *elicitation*. The student used the third person singular after the modal verb 'can'; the base form of the verb 'run' should have been used instead. The teacher in this example uses a repetition and then asks the student to complete the sentence again with the correct form ('The cat can runs? The cat can … '). The fifth exchange is an example of *repetition*. The student used the incorrect form of the plural of 'child', *'childs'. The teacher, in this case, repeats what the student has just said, using question intonation to draw attention to the form. Exchange six is an example of a *recast*. The student uses the object pronoun 'her' instead of the reflexive pronoun 'herself'. The teacher reformulates what was said, minus the error, in 'Oh. Mary made the cake by herself.'

Lyster and Ranta (1997) found that the most frequent of these moves is the recast, and other studies have also shown recasts to be the most common type of feedback provided by L2 teachers (for example, Simard & Jean, 2011; Zyzik & Polio, 2008). However, Lyster (2004) found that students in content-based French immersion classes seldom responded to teacher recasts, and the corrections teachers made tended not to be taken up by learners. The feedback types that more often led to student self-correction were ones that drew students' attention to the forms and also required some response from the student. Following these kinds of feedback, students were more likely to take up the correct form in subsequent usage than following recasts. The crucial feature of feedback to learners is whether learners actively focus on and engage in use of the language. Throughout this book, we will illustrate how interaction and negotiation of meaning can support a focus on form.

Students need multiple opportunities to encounter and engage with forms and meanings in meaningful contexts of use (Spada & Lightbown, 1993, 1999). Classroom learning offers excellent opportunities for such encounters and engagement, as topics are developed over multiple lessons and content is repeatedly revisited. The language students work with as they learn school subjects offers them optimal opportunities for this frequent focus and supports learning language and content simultaneously. This is demonstrated in Harley's (1998) experimental study of children in six Grade 2 French immersion classrooms who were encouraged to focus on gender marking of French nouns. The research found that the children succeeded better in learning gender marking when they worked with language clearly related to the themes the teachers were developing in their subject area teaching, compared to when the words were presented in activities without any thematic thread and congruity with the curriculum. It is this kind of proactive/planned grammar instruction in authentic discourse contexts that this book advocates. Spotlight Study 2.1 is another example:

Spotlight Study 2.1

Doughty and Varela (1998) conducted an experimental form-focused study of middle school science classrooms that investigated the effects of recasts requiring learner repetition of the correct forms. They found that students who were given feedback on their use of past tense and conditional constructions improved their accuracy in using these forms. The target forms were frequent in the talk and writing the students needed to do to learn science, and a focus on the forms helped students state their hypotheses and report their results with greater precision.

In this study, 34 middle school students from two ESL science classes were divided into a control group and a treatment group to explore the impact of teacher recasting that repeated the student's error and modeled the correct form for the student to repeat. The forms chosen for the study were identified in discussion between the researchers and the teacher, who had recognized that the students had difficulty with the past time reference and conditional expressions needed to write up science experiments. The researchers tested the students on these features before the study began and then tested them again at the end. There was no instruction in these features during the study.

To conduct the experiment, the teacher in the treatment classroom consistently drew attention to past tense and conditional errors in students' speech and writing. In the spoken language in the classroom, she provided corrective recasts by repeating the error with rising intonation, and then recasting the utterance to model the target form. For example:

José: I think that the worm will go under the soil.
Teacher: I *think* that the worm *will* go under the soil?
José: (no response)
Teacher: I *thought* that the worm *would* go under the soil.
José: I *thought* that the worm *would* go under the soil.

(Doughty & Varela, 1998, p. 124)

In addition, students were given **corrective feedback** on these forms in their written work when they made errors. The treatment group improved substantially on the accuracy with which they used these forms in speech and writing, far beyond the control group. The treatment group also used more past tense forms. Two months later, the treatment group improvement still endured. Moreover, those learners began to self-correct, showing that their awareness of these features was heightened by the treatment. ■

One aspect of this work that is of particular interest to us is that the teacher in the study was initially reluctant to correct students' errors. She wanted the focus to stay on science, and was concerned about the impact of the correction on the classroom dynamics and students' learning of content. What convinced her to participate in the study was her realization that the grammatical features in focus in the study were important for doing science. By being more precise and accurate in their hypotheses and reports, the students were achieving greater proficiency both in language use and in learning science.

But the teacher did experience some challenges in providing this kind of reactive feedback and found that it impacted and influenced classroom dynamics in different ways. For example, students were disturbed if the teacher's response only corrected the grammar and did not attend to meaning. The teacher had to continually remind herself to pay attention both to the meaning the students were presenting and to the form, as focusing on form could be distracting from the focus on meaning. In addition, the teacher found that she had to limit the number of corrections directed to any particular student, as students sometimes became frustrated with the recasting and repetition. And finally, the teacher had to recognize when correction was appropriate and when not. In panel presentations by the students, for example, the teacher found that correction was disruptive and sometimes embarrassing. Overall, however, the students were open to the recasting and reported that it made them focus both on what they were saying and on how they were saying it.

Doughty and Varela's study shows how a focus on form can be made relevant to the content classroom by drawing learners' attention to grammar when they are using the forms in completing classroom work. It demonstrates the need for **proactive** as well as **reactive focus on form**, and provides support for prompting and elicitation techniques that go beyond simple recasting and lead to the production of language. These are issues we will continue to address as we discuss ways of teaching grammar in Chapters 3 and 4 that enable a focus on meaning and form.

Later in this chapter, we introduce a slightly different definition of the recast in presenting the framework from Gibbons (2006a) that will contribute to the discussion of grammar teaching in Chapters 3 and 4. The point here is that the results of this research on form-focused instruction show the importance of engaging the learner and bringing explicit attention to language itself in ways that prompt learner responses. This research helps us think about the purpose of grammar teaching not just as correcting errors but also as building students' language resources for meaning-making.

The Role of Metalanguage

The research we have reviewed thus far shows the importance of interaction, focused attention requiring response and engagement of learners, and the need for multiple exposures to and production of the language to be learned. In addition, the approach presented in the next chapters is based on the idea that in order to generalize about language and help learners understand the language systems they are drawing on, a teacher needs a language for talking about language. A metalanguage provides a means of focusing on wording in the texts students read and write, and of engaging in talk about that wording.

Harley (1998) shows that even children aged seven and eight can use some metalanguage to talk about the language they are learning. In this study of proactive form-focused instruction, children participated in games and other age-appropriate activities designed to draw their attention to the indicators of noun gender in French, where nouns are marked as masculine or feminine. This is an issue that is very challenging for learners and is often a continuing problem in French immersion contexts, according to Harley. Interviews she conducted with these children in her study show how the metalanguage 'masculine' and 'feminine' was taken up by the students as they reported on the explicit knowledge about grammar they had developed:

Interviewer:	*Tout à l'heure tu as dit 'le biberon jaune'. Est-ce que tu peux me dire pourquoi tu as dit 'LE biberon'?* [Just now you said *le biberon jaune* (the yellow baby's bottle). Can you tell me why you said *LE biberon* (THE (M) baby's bottle)?]
Student:	*Um. Parce que c'est 'on' et c'est toujours masculin quand c'est 'on'.* [Um. Because it's *on* and it's always masculine when it's *on*.]
Interviewer:	*OK. Bien.* [OK. Good.]
Student:	*Uh, pas 'la maison'.* [Uh, not *la maison* (the (F) house).]
Interviewer:	*Pas 'la maison', OK.* [Not la maison, OK.]

(Harley, 1998, p. 168)

In this book, we will show how the use of a grammatical metalanguage can be a resource for helping students learn grammar in context and for bringing form into focus through meaningful language use that also addresses broader curricular goals.

Most teachers are familiar with traditional metalanguage such as *verb*, *noun*, *conjunction*, and *present tense*. This book also introduces some functional metalanguage. Learning to use new metalanguage is a skill in itself that needs to be taught in order to enable students to use it to talk about the language of the texts they read and write. But to be meaningful, the learning of metalanguage needs to be situated in instructional contexts where it resonates with and helps support content goals. Research in L1 and L2 education and writing instruction shows that just learning linguistic terminology is not in itself supportive of other learning goals (Myhill, 2003; Svalberg, 2007). So while being explicit about language requires metalanguage, use of metalanguage does not in itself necessarily support connections to meaning. Berry (2010) points out that metalanguage can be thought of as both thing (terminology) and process (talk about language). In this book, we will show how teachers can situate talk about language within content teaching and use it in the service of their larger instructional goals. Interaction using metalanguage supports students in looking closely at language to see patterns that can be linked with categories of meaning.

Classroom Snapshot 2.2

Schleppegrell (2013) offers an example from a Grade 2 mainstream classroom with a majority of English language learners, where the teacher has asked the children to work in groups to identify what she refers to as 'doing processes'. The children have learned to identify doing processes in verb phrases that present actions. The class is reading the story *Julius* by Angela Johnson. The teacher's goal is to contrast what Julius, a pig, does early in the story and what he does after he has learned some manners. Julius is introduced in this way by the author:

> But it was a pig. A big pig. An Alaskan pig, who did a polar bear imitation and climbed out of the crate.

(Johnson, 1993, no page numbers)

One group of children has highlighted 'did a polar bear imitation'. The teacher asks the whole class if the group was right to highlight that part. The students give differing opinions, some responding 'no'. The teacher asks, 'Who's saying no and why do you think not?' A student replies, 'Cuz he wasn't a polar bear – he was a pig.' The teacher and class then enter into a discussion about the meaning of 'imitate' and 'imitation'. They talk about other kinds of imitating and about their own experiences of imitating. Finally, the teacher asks again, 'So do you think he did something here? Or no?' Together, the children say 'He did' (p. 162).

Examining representations of characters' actions and using the metalanguage *doing process* enables students to pay close attention to language and meaning. The metalanguage has enabled recognition that 'did a polar bear imitation' was indeed an action, as the metalinguistic labeling drew attention to form and meaning. ■

This kind of metalanguage and metatalk enables learners to recognize patterns in the ways the new language presents meanings and helps them begin to recognize the choices they can make in the new language. Because functional grammar metalanguage like *doing process* connects to meaning, using such talk about language enables discussion about what a character does, says, and thinks. It also equips learners to discuss how characters are described and how they evolve across a text. In that way, the metalanguage also supports curricular goals by offering a means of being explicit about how language presents the knowledge to be learned (Schleppegrell, 2013). The use of functional metalanguage in the context of curricular activities to help students notice and attend to form has been shown to support even young children in expanding their meaning-making resources (Williams, 2004, 2005; French, 2010). In this book, we focus primarily on research that shows how functional metalanguage can promote talk about the meaning in texts typical of school contexts: the stories read and arguments written in Language Arts, the history textbook, and the reports written in science. The metalanguage helps students recognize that an author's linguistic choices are consequential for the meanings made in a text, and analysis of these choices helps students learn how the grammar of the language works.

Functional Grammar: Focus on Grammar and Meaning

As discussed in Chapter 1, what we mean by learning 'grammar' in this book is the development of language resources for accomplishing the goals of schooling. The theory of language that provides a foundation for this conceptualization of grammar comes from the linguistic theory of Michael Halliday, **systemic functional linguistics (SFL)**. (For accessible introductions to SFL, see Butt, Fahey, Feez, & Spinks, 2012, or Humphrey, Droga, & Feez, 2012. For an introduction that links functional and traditional grammar, see Derewianka, 2011, and Droga & Humphrey, 2003). This approach to teaching grammar is explicit in its focus on language and in linking form and meaning. However, language is addressed not through responses to errors and explicit teaching of grammar rules, but instead through a focus on how language is used in text and discourse and how meanings are presented in the language used in teaching and learning. This does not mean that teachers should not respond to errors or teach grammar rules, but these aspects of grammar teaching are not the main concern of this book. Instead, we offer here a framework for connecting language forms and meaning in contexts of use, recognizing grammar as a resource for meaning-making. This gives us a principled approach to grammar instruction while focusing on the content to be learned in primary and secondary classroom activities. It makes it possible for teachers to be explicit about language forms at the same time as they emphasize meaning, and to offer an explicit pedagogy that affords grammar a central role.

From a functional grammar perspective, learning grammar means learning the options that are available in the new language to make meanings of different kinds. It means learning new ways of using language to accomplish particular social purposes. A functional focus on grammar allows L2 learners to become aware of the meaning in different language choices, in oral and written language. Teachers engage L2 learners in talking about the grammatical choices of speakers and writers, giving them opportunities to develop knowledge about how language is used to make particular meanings in particular contexts.

Functional grammar activities offer techniques for teaching about language. They help readers tackle a text by recognizing how groups of words work together in different parts of a sentence, and by seeing how these sentence parts are related to each other. You will learn how to guide readers to unpack dense and complex phrases, identify what is described and defined, explore actions and who is involved in them, and track referents across a text. You will focus on logical connectors and conjunctions to help students see patterns in language. You will develop a language for talking about language that helps young readers see the meaning in the ways authors create texts of various kinds.

From a pedagogical perspective, this view of grammar and approach to teaching grammar suggests a focus on close analysis of the language used in different situations, supported by classroom discussion about why authors use specific language choices to achieve certain effects. We will see throughout this book many examples of research that takes this functional grammar approach. For instance, Gibbons (2003, 2006a) investigated how teacher–student talk in a science classroom contributes to learners' language development. Specifically, she explored ways in which teacher and students co-constructed meaning and how the teacher built bridges between the everyday language of L2 learners and the academic language of science.

The key theoretical principle underlying the SFL grammar is the idea that any time we use language, we are simultaneously presenting ideas and enacting a relationship with the listener or reader. As we do both of those things, we also need to construct a cohesive message. Grammar can be examined from each of these three angles: how language is used to present ideas, enact a relationship, and construct a cohesive message. These are discussed in turn below with examples and illustrations.

Presenting Ideas

In terms of presenting ideas, we focus on the content of the message, looking at what information is contributed by the nouns, verbs, prepositional phrases, and adverbs. In this book, much of the research we discuss uses the functional grammar terms **participant**, **process**, and **circumstance** to refer to these language forms. *Participants* are the nouns and noun groups; *processes* are presented in the verbs and verb groups; and *circumstances* are presented in the prepositional phrases and adverbs. The functional metalanguage lets us look at the parts of a sentence not just as individual words but also as meaningful phrases. The labels make it possible to quickly identify the parts of the sentence that go together. So, for example, rather than using traditional metalanguage to label each word in a sentence, we can use the functional metalanguage to identify its meaningful units. This is illustrated in Figure 2.1.

Identifying the meaningful units helps us recognize the contribution of each group of words to the overall meaning in the sentence. Processes show what is going on: the *doing, thinking, saying,* or *being* (Martin & Rose, 2003). Participants refer to who or what is participating in the process, represented as person(s) or thing(s). The circumstances surrounding events are the *when, where, how,* and *why* of the process.

In Chapters 3 and 4, you will learn more about the different process types and how you can use a focus on process types to support L2 learners in recognizing the differences in the ways history, science, and Language Arts texts typically present information. By thinking about the verbs and verb phrases in terms of whether they are expressing doing, thinking/ feeling, saying, or being, you develop tools for thinking about the kinds of information and experience students encounter in texts in different

My favorite experience last summer was a trip to the mountains.

Traditional metalanguage analysis:

My	favorite	experience	last	summer	was	a	trip	to	the	mountains.
Det	*Adj*	*Noun*	*Adj*	*Noun*	*Verb*	*Det*	*Noun*	*Prep*	*Det*	*Noun*

Functional metalanguage analysis:

My favorite experience	last summer	was	a trip to the mountains.
Participant	*Circumstance*	*Process*	*Participant*

Figure 2.1 Analyzing a sentence using traditional and functional metalanguage

subjects and different tasks. You can also recognize changes in the ways texts present information as children move through the school years. For example, you will see that as students move into secondary school, the being processes (also called *relational processes*) become more prominent. This is because students more frequently read and write about abstract and theoretical concepts rather than the actions and feelings that tend to be more prominent in primary school texts. This has implications for the grammar that is most useful to incorporate into teaching at those different levels.

In Chapters 3 and 4, you will see how a focus on process types can help learners develop strategies for comprehension. You will see how deconstructing a text into its processes, participants, circumstances, and connectors can help learners see how language works to make meaning in different subject areas. In Chapter 4, you will learn about more participants, including nominalizations and complex noun groups. These are common features of secondary school texts, as they enable the abstraction, evaluation, and theorizing that emerge in the texts of the later years of schooling.

Here, let's see what students can learn from analyzing the circumstances in a text:

Activity 2.2

The text below, from *Urban Roosts* by Barbara Bash, is an informational text about city birds and where they live, taken from a primary school Language Arts curriculum. Identify the circumstances of time and place in the text, and consider what children would learn about language by doing this.

> One familiar urban dweller is the pigeon. Long ago it was called a rock dove, because it lived in the rocky cliffs along the coast of Europe. Today it flourishes all over the United States in the nooks and crannies of our cities.
>
> (Bash, 1990, no page numbers)

The circumstances of place include 'in the rocky cliffs along the coast of Europe' and 'all over the United States in the nooks and crannies of our cities'. These circumstances of place describe where the pigeons used to live and where they live now. The circumstances of time are 'Long ago' and 'Today'. Children can identify these and see that by beginning the sentences with circumstances of time, the author contrasts the two time periods. They can then see how circumstances of place indicate what was different for pigeons in these time periods.

The deconstruction of sentences into processes, participants, and circumstances, as we will see in the following chapters, offers a strategy for focusing on meaning by identifying the words that go together to make meanings in a clause. As teachers and students work together to explore sentences in this way, in the context of reading a text or preparing to write, they engage in talk about the choices an author has made and simultaneously focus on form and content, learning more about how the language resources are used for meaning-making.

Enacting a Relationship with the Reader or Listener

In every use of language, we draw on grammatical systems that indicate the kind of relationship we are enacting: whether it is formal or informal, close or distant, and whether it is shaped by attitudes of various kinds. This means not just focusing on the meaning of nouns, verbs, and other structures but also exploring the grammatical choices that support interaction and exchange of meanings. For example, Classroom Snapshot 1.1 illustrated how a teacher was asking her class to identify declarative, interrogative, and imperative mood in English and exploring the speech functions they present. This engaged students in conversation about how we use different grammatical choices when we 'command' each other to do things in different contexts. In Chapter 3, you will explore this interaction more closely.

In addition to choices from the mood system, **modality** is another grammatical resource that can be in focus for exploring interpersonal meaning. The two major areas of modal meaning are *probability* and *obligation*, and modality is presented in modal verbs, adjuncts, and even nouns. For example, the modality of probability is expressed through all of these forms:

- modal verbs: 'might', 'could', etc.
- modal adjuncts: 'maybe', 'certainly', etc.
- modal meaning in nouns: 'possibility', 'requirement', 'potential', etc.

By examining these and other forms of representing probability, learners can explore the resources offered in English for taking an intermediate stance. (For more on this area of meaning, see, for example, Lock, 1996).

Constructing a Cohesive Message

Some language choices are not about presenting content or enacting a relationship, but instead serve to construct a message that holds together and builds from clause to clause. For example, conjunctions build relationships between parts of the clause or text, and reference is constructed in cohesive ties presented in pronouns, demonstratives, and synonyms, among other linguistic resources.

In this book, *connector* refers to a conjunction or other linking phrase that creates **cohesion** and a logical development across a text. Figure 2.2 presents examples of connectors and the areas of meaning they contribute to.

Meaning	Example connectors
Addition	*and, and then, furthermore*
Comparison/contrast	*but, for example, instead, in other words, however, in fact*
Time	*when, then*
Cause/consequence	*because, so, despite, nevertheless, even though*
Condition	*if, unless*
Purpose	*in order to, so*
Sequence	*first, second, finally*

Figure 2.2 Connectors

In Chapters 3 and 4, you will explore the role of connectors and conjunctions to see how a focus on them can help children and adolescents analyze the overall structure of a text. You will read about classroom activities that helped learners use conjunctions to make their persuasive writing more authoritative and effective.

We also show how students' attention can be drawn to the way cohesion is created through reference ties. Figure 2.3 presents information about reference devices. You will learn to track reference across a text and see how that enables learners to recognize connections and the evolution of meaning.

These three aspects of the ways grammar makes meaning—through presenting ideas, enacting a relationship, and constructing a cohesive message—are referred to from the SFL perspective as *metafunctions*. They are the overarching functions language performs as it helps us engage in and shape our interactions with others. The SFL metalanguage offers us different approaches to a text, with one or the other of these metafunctions in focus as we explore the various kinds of meanings presented by different language resources.

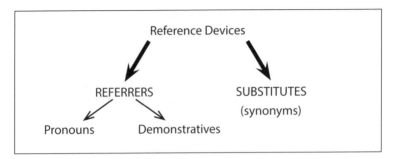

Reference devices are words that stand for other words in a text. Here are some common reference devices:

- *Referrers* refer back to a noun used in a previous clause or refer forward to a noun or noun group appearing in the next clause. Referrers can be *pronouns* (such as *itself, its, they*) or *demonstratives* (for example, *this, that, these, those*).
- *Substitutes* are synonyms that appear together with other referrers or as single words that stand for a concept that has been or will be introduced. (If substitutes are not used, the text becomes very repetitive.) Substitutes may appear together with referrers, as in the following text:

> To protect Spanish claims, King Carlos ordered that settlements be built in Alta California.
> (…)
> King Carlos gave **this order** after **he** heard that Russia had set up a colony in Alaska. **The king** worried that Russian fur traders would move south from Alaska. **They** might try to set up a colony in California.
>
> (Boehm et al., 2000, p. 142)

- *This* is a demonstrative and *order* is a substitute for *King Carlos ordered that settlements be built in Alta California.*
- *He* is a pronoun that refers back to *King Carlos.*
- *The king* is a substitute for *King Carlos.*
- *They* is a pronoun that refers back to *Russian fur traders.*

Figure 2.3 Reference devices (adapted from Schleppegrell & de Oliveira, 2006)

This book also draws on traditional grammatical metalanguage, and offers ways of bridging between the traditional and functional metalanguage in support of readers who are more familiar with traditional terminology. We hope the introduction of some functional metalanguage offers additional pedagogical resources for focusing on form and meaning in contexts of use.

SFL is a complex linguistic theory, and our purpose here is not to teach about SFL, but instead to share insights from it that have informed recent L2 instruction based on research findings about how languages are best learned. These studies show that SFL's functional grammar provides tools for the kind of focus on form and meaning in context that research shows facilitates and supports L2 development. Spotlight Study 2.2 is an example.

Spotlight Study 2.2

Aguirre-Muñoz, Park, Amabisca, and Boscardin (2008) provide evidence that teachers can use a functional grammar perspective to provide feedback to L2 learners in ways that are effective in improving their writing. Their study was prompted by a concern that sheltered instruction was not providing the challenging content needed in the Language Arts classroom as English language learners in California engaged in academic writing and response to literature. The researchers developed an intervention based in SFL for 21 mainstream middle school teachers who had significant numbers of ELLs in their classrooms. Their intervention was designed to increase teachers' understanding of academic language features so they could be more explicit with students in their feedback on writing.

They provided teachers and students with a framework and a set of linguistic tools for examining text, for exploring content in the texts they read, and for talking about valued grammatical features of writing assignments. Through classroom talk, the teachers focused students' attention on how characters and events were presented in literature by the authors they were reading, looking at the ways characters were described and evaluated. In their writing about literature, students used the same language features to expand noun phrases describing characters, objects, and places. Teachers reported that this helped students move beyond referring to characters only with pronouns and proper nouns. Teachers also raised students' awareness of how conjunctions and transitional phrases are used and the different kinds of verbs used in literature to create more interesting text. This helped students produce more varied and better structured sentences, and achieve clearer cohesion across their texts.

Following the intervention, the researchers looked at how training in linguistic features influenced teachers' evaluation of student work and its impact on instructional practices. They found that teachers were able to talk with students about 'grammatical structures that build cohesion, vocabulary that reveals interpretation, long noun phrases that increase sentence variety, and overall essay cohesion and organization' (p. 12). ■

The form of grammar teaching we highlight in this book calls for talk about language in context using functional metalanguage. This enables discussion that supports content learning more generally, helping learners notice language features that also present the subject-matter knowledge they need to learn. This book will introduce you to ways of talking about such grammatical features as noun group expansion, conjunctions, cohesive reference, and other resources for meaning-making. As you encounter teachers engaging students in reflecting on and talking about grammar in Chapters 3 and 4, you will consider how their actions and activities support what is important for L2 development.

A Developmental Progression in Learning Grammar

Students in many educational settings learn language and content at the same time (Lightbown, 2014; Lindholm-Leary & Borsato, 2006; Lyster, 2007; Snow, 1998; Snow, Met, & Genesee, 1989). A key issue for teachers in second language contexts is how to support students in learning both language and content as they participate in classroom instruction. Situating grammar instruction in the context of learning school subjects offers learners opportunities for the frequent exposure, focus on form and meaning, and conscious attention to language needed for success. A content-embedded grammar teaching approach is also supported by theories of learning and language development more generally (for example, Vygotsky, 1986). Language develops through interaction, and as students engage with new concepts, instruction in grammar provides additional insights into the choices they can make from the language they are learning to speak and write in ways that help them achieve the goals of schooling.

The grammar points foregrounded in this book come from and support the reading, writing, and oral language activities of the mainstream classroom and grade-level contexts. The grammar activities described in the research reported in Chapters 3 and 4 help students understand how the choices a speaker or author makes result in particular effects and differences in meaning. The activities presented there also illustrate how a teaching syllabus for grammar cannot simply list grammatical structures to be learned. Since structures are not learned one by one in a linear way (Ellis & Larsen-Freeman, 2006; Lightbown & Spada, 2013), the grammar in focus needs to be drawn from the contexts in which it is encountered in the school curriculum.

Although a list of structures cannot form the basis of a grammar syllabus, there is a language developmental progression that teachers need to be aware of when working with children in school. Based on her analysis of thousands of texts written by students across the school years and subject areas, Frances Christie (2012) describes a progression that school learners follow in the development of their L1 grammar. This progression is also helpful for thinking about the challenges in L2 learning. In both L1 and L2 development, children typically learn how to talk in here-and-now contexts where they can see who they are speaking to and in which there are visuals, gestures, and body language. When they go to school and develop literacy skills, children learn to use language in more abstract ways to refer to things and events that are not in their immediate surroundings or part of their shared experience (Gibbons, 2002). That means they have to draw on new language resources to express generalization or abstraction (Gibbons, 2006a). In this context, teachers need to create shared experiences of language use that highlight the new linguistic resources and give students practice in using them.

Over the school years, the nature of the experiences that students engage with changes. Increasingly, they work with disciplinary texts that present meanings more remote from the activities of daily life (for example, as they conduct and report on research in history or science, or as they analyze and reflect on literary texts in English). This calls for a growing attention to the grammar typical of written language in order to deal with the knowledge, experience, and ideas of the disciplinary discourses of the subject areas. This kind of language has been characterized as *academic language* or *the language of schooling* (Cummins & Man, 2007; Schleppegrell, 2004).

Christie shows how talk about grammar can support students in moving toward control of increasingly dense and abstract language and developing more advanced forms of expression. She describes how children initially draw on their oral language resources as they begin to move into the written mode in developing literacy. Movement toward the written mode involves learning about the grammatical organization of written language, with information more densely packed into sentences, and developing new ways of expressing attitude and evaluation to present generalizations and abstract ideas. The frameworks provided by Gibbons and Christie help us understand what might productively be in focus in the primary school years and what language forms are important to comprehend and produce in secondary school. By recognizing that language in the written mode and in the tasks of schooling requires new forms of grammatical expression, teachers can help learners build the language resources that enable the new kinds of meaning-making needed to develop new knowledge. For children learning language at school, the focus on grammar can be situated in every subject area and infused throughout curricular activities. This is the approach taken in this book. Chapters 3 and 4 will further explore research on ways of raising students' awareness of those language forms.

Activity 2.3

Compare these sentences from students' writing. Try to put them into the age order you think they reflect. What helps you make your decision?

- 'When the apples were all picked, Laura and I got to go to a movie.'
- 'We went to the beach.'
- 'My favorite experience last summer was a trip to the mountains.'
- 'Last weekend my friend and I rode our bikes to the lake.'

These four sentences are different in structure and in the amount of information they contain. They reflect the kind of growth in control of language that we expect of children as they mature. 'We went to the beach' is a typical way early writers might draw on the grammar of English. They use pronouns ('we') without having introduced the participants in the activity, relying on context or shared knowledge for the reference to be clear. This sentence also omits any information about the time of the activity. 'Last weekend my friend and I rode our bikes to the lake' shows development in control of the language, as the writer now uses an introductory circumstance of time to provide a temporal reference for the action and identifies the second participant as 'my friend'. 'When the apples were all picked, we got to go to a movie' shows the development of further complexity, as the writer joins two clauses in a relationship of time, linking two actions. Finally, 'My favorite experience last summer was a trip to the mountains' is written by an older student who is able to draw on the grammar and vocabulary of English to construct a sentence that both presents and evaluates an event, described in an abstract form, calling it 'my favorite experience'.

These examples present a simplified view of the language development a teacher might expect to see. However, it is this kind of development of L2 abilities that we focus on in this book. We indicate how, through specific types of interaction, teachers can help students realize the meaning-making potential of the language and learn new ways of speaking and writing. This perspective also means that learners don't need to be restricted to simplified texts; instead they can work with texts and tasks appropriate to their age and cognitive levels of development. This only becomes possible if teachers have the resources to help students see how language works, deconstruct the texts they read, and make choices in their writing.

Grammar instruction is needed at all levels of L2 language proficiency. Beginners can benefit from explicit attention to linguistic forms that they will then be aware of as they continue learning (Ellis, 2005). Advanced learners, such as many language learners in our schools, need attention to grammar in order to participate in challenging tasks at school. This book offers multiple examples of ways of being explicit about grammar instruction in contexts of authentic, age-appropriate classroom learning, as teachers and students engage with and talk about the language of the texts they are reading and writing. Talk about written language has the advantage that the grammar in focus can be analyzed, unpacked, and explored, giving students opportunities to practice using the language in new ways.

A Framework for Grammar Instruction: Gibbons' Mode-Shifting Moves

In Chapter 3, you will learn more about Pauline Gibbons' (2006a) important research with L2 children in the context of science instruction. Here, we want to introduce her work as well as a set of issues she highlights that will remain in focus for us as we look into primary and secondary school classrooms. Gibbons offers us the construct **mode continuum** to help us think about how the language resources students draw on shift in expected ways as they move from face-to-face interaction into retelling experience, reporting on what they have learned, and writing texts appropriate to different school subjects and genres.

The mode continuum refers to movement between spoken and written language as well as to movement between more everyday and more technical language. Gibbons suggests that shifting back and forth across the mode continuum assists L2 students in drawing on what they can already do with language and supports them in expanding their meaning-making resources into new areas. To evaluate the ways teachers facilitate this movement, she suggests four **pedagogical moves** that enable teachers and students to make shifts across the oral/written as well as formal/informal continua and support students in adapting their language to context:

1 'talking about language, using meaningful metalanguage'
2 'unpacking written language'
3 'recasting student discourse'
4 'reminding and handing over'.

(Gibbons, 2006a, pp. 125–6)

For Gibbons, 'talking about language, using meaningful metalanguage' means bringing to students' attention the linguistic resources they need to accomplish their purposes in a particular task. For example, in preparing her students for writing about magnetism, the teacher says, 'I want you to tell me what you *know* about magnets from this ... it would be something that happens *always* so we would write it in the *present* tense' (Gibbons 2006a, p. 136). Here, the metalanguage of 'present tense' is connected with its function in enabling presentation of timeless meaning in the context of writing about something that always happens. This talk about how language works enables the teacher to make generalizations about grammar that help students make effective choices in their writing.

'Unpacking written language' is a means of moving back and forth along the mode continuum, taking something that is written and restating it in ways that are more everyday or informal. Chapters 3 and 4 provide examples of students and teachers working together to unpack the language of textbooks or other written texts by identifying grammatical constituents and talking about their role within the larger text and discourse.

Gibbons' use of the term 'recast' is somewhat different from the way it has been described within the form-focused research literature. For Gibbons, recasting means responding to student-initiated topics by restating their contributions in more authoritative, technical, or disciplinary discourse. It does not refer just to reformulating a learner's incorrect utterance. For example, a fifth grade student, in reporting on hands-on group-work with magnets, says: 'I thought that all metal can stick on magnets but when I tried it some of them they didn't stick.' The teacher recasts this as: 'OK, so you thought that no matter what object, if it was a metal object it would be attracted to the magnet' (Gibbons, 2006a, pp. 126–7). This recasts both the form and the meaning, with the focus on helping the student learn the technical language needed to talk authoritatively about magnetism and demonstrate her knowledge in ways that will be recognized as 'scientific'.

'Reminding and handing over' is an alternative to recasting: rather than restating what a student has said, the teacher simply prompts the students to reformulate what they have said themselves. This echoes Lyster's (2004) distinction between recasting and prompting, reviewed above, that suggests students benefit more from prompting in the long term. Reminding and handing over is a step toward giving learners increased responsibility and diminishing the amount of scaffolding provided by the teacher. It typically occurs after the students have built up metalinguistic knowledge and is also a means of assessing students' learning.

All of these moves support students in gaining facility with the language—in learning grammar. In Chapters 3 and 4, you will have the opportunity to evaluate instances of teacher–student interaction in terms of these moves.

Summary

Research has clearly supported the view that a focus on form should be integrated into a language teaching program (for example, Doughty & Williams, 1998; Ellis, 2002; Norris & Ortega, 2000, 2009; Spada, 2010), especially when the learners have the goal of developing literacy and using the language being learned in academic or professional contexts. Children learning an L2 in school are often learning the language not only for its own sake but also to engage in literacy tasks and content learning. When children are learning second or foreign languages at school, they need to do more than build their conversational and interactional skills. They need to be able to learn content appropriate for their developmental levels through the new language. The focus of grammar instruction, then, is most appropriately on *development*, helping learners expand their meaning-making repertoires. As they do so, they inevitably make new errors. That makes it important to recognize that growth in learning grammar is not just about correctness of form.

In this chapter, we have presented the theoretical perspectives that inform the approach to grammar instruction you will encounter in the next chapters. The approaches to L2 grammar teaching we have discussed recognize the social and developmental nature of L2 learning and situate grammar teaching in meaningful contexts of learning relevant to the goals of schooling. The sociocultural and functional linguistics perspectives developed here underlie the activities and pedagogical moves you will explore in primary and secondary classrooms as you read Chapters 3 and 4. The pedagogical moves presented in the research in these chapters can help you focus students' attention on language and enable the noticing and awareness-raising that promote L2 development.

The following chapters illustrate how guided focus on language through the learning of school subjects can raise students' consciousness about how language works. Chapters 3 and 4 report on research that illustrates how teachers can expand learners' language resources by drawing their attention to the use of particular structures and the meaning-making choices available in different contexts of use. These chapters describe the role of the teacher in grammar instruction, and reinforce the importance of *noticing* in language development. The activities they describe provide learners with experiences of exploring language use in important social contexts. Such noticing, discussion about language form, and social interaction help learners understand the choices they can make from systems of the new language, as well as affording practice in negotiating choice of form and meaning in context.

3

Classroom-Based Research on Grammar: Young Children

Preview

In Chapter 2, we reviewed theory and research that informs our understanding about how best to teach grammar in meaningful ways in second language classrooms. This research confirms that L2 learners need opportunities for explicit attention to grammar in meaningful contexts to help them engage in the noticing and awareness-raising that support language development. In this chapter, we will report on research that has investigated the teaching and learning of L2 grammar in second language learning contexts at the primary school level.

What Do Students Need to Learn about Grammar in Primary School?

As the review of teaching and learning L2 grammar presented in Chapter 2 showed, grammar needs to be taught in meaningful contexts to facilitate L2 learning. The theory of language development discussed in that chapter suggests that L2 learners need to notice grammatical forms and recognize their roles in meaning-making. Neither a focus solely on form nor a focus solely on meaning is sufficient in helping children engage with and use the complex language expected in participating in school subjects. Children who are learning languages at school are usually also learning something else. In immersion or mainstream classrooms, where they are learning the content of the subject-matter curriculum, grammar teaching and learning can be infused into classroom teaching in all subject areas. In foreign language classrooms, or in second language classrooms where learning the language is the primary goal, teachers still need to choose communicative contexts for language learning. In such settings, the context for grammar instruction might be games and activities which focus on communication. Teachers of children everywhere know that language cannot be taught in isolation from its use. This book shows how grammar teaching can be situated in meaningful contexts of use where it supports L2 development by focusing on the expansion of L2 learners' grammatical resources, not just on accuracy in producing specific grammatical forms.

Some readers may question whether primary-school-aged children are capable of learning grammar. Grammar calls for an ability to think about abstractions and categories, and some might wonder whether children in the early grades are ready for this kind of classroom work. But current theories of child development, based on the work of Vygotsky (1986), recognize that even young children are able to—and even enjoy—thinking about language and how it works, and that they are capable of working with abstractions. Vygotsky (1986) points out that much of what children learn in school is conscious awareness of what they do and that '[g]rammar and writing help the child to rise to a higher level of speech development' (p. 184). Children are capable of abstract understandings about grammar even at an early age, as research by Williams (2005) and French (2010, 2012) has shown. In their research in primary school classrooms with a mix of L1 and L2 students, they found that a meaningful focus on grammar helped primary grade students build their awareness of how language works. In arguing for a functional grammar approach with young children, French (2010) concludes that engaging them with grammar is a means of supporting their development of abstraction: 'If children are given appropriate intellectual tools and support, more abstract thinking is made possible' (p. 227). One such tool, as we will see below, is grammatical metalanguage that helps students think about language and meaning.

This chapter starts by discussing how teachers can decide what to focus on, using the notion of mode shifting and through the identification of language that helps children do different things at different points in the unit of instruction, as described in Chapter 2. Then the chapter explores how teachers can proactively raise awareness of grammar at the primary level. Examples from different contexts and content areas are used to show how grammar can be integrated in classroom instruction.

Chapter 1 defined grammar as the full set of language resources through which meaning is presented. Viewing grammar in this way focuses attention on the patterns of language that students encounter across the years of schooling, starting in primary school, in both L1 and L2 learning. Expanding grammatical resources in the context of schooling means helping children develop language that enables their participation in the tasks expected of them in classroom activities.

In Chapter 1, we presented a way of thinking about grammar teaching across a unit of instruction. Let's apply that here to a classroom where a teacher of L2 students wants to support their language development as they learn mathematics.

Activity 3.1

Imagine you are a fifth grade teacher who wants to provide language support as you teach your L2 learners how to divide fractions. You are not sure what grammar to focus on. In your teaching, you use artifacts and visuals and engage students in hands-on group activities that help them understand fractions. You typically have them report on the group-work through oral presentations. Then you usually ask them to write about how to solve the problem. You also use the mathematics textbook explanations.

Table 3.1 shows four examples ('texts') of the kind of language that students encounter and engage in as they learn mathematics. The students are working on the following problem:

> Ms. Stangle wants to make peach tarts for her friends. She needs two-thirds of a peach for each tart and she has 10 peaches. What is the greatest number of tarts that she can make with 10 peaches?
>
> (Chapin, O'Connor, & Anderson, 2003, p. 31)

Text 1	S1: Mark it like this … S2: No, try this way. S1: OK, count those … 30. S2: The tarts all need two. Thirty divided by two. S1: Fifteen.
Text 2	We drew the ten peaches and then cut each one into three parts. Then we counted all the parts. So it was 30 parts, and each tart had to have two parts, so we divided 30 by two and got 15 tarts.
Text 3	When you want to find how many thirds there are, you can divide each of the ten peaches into three. When you count how many thirds there are in total, you get 30. Since each tart needs two thirds, you can divide 30 by two and get 15. That means that Ms. Stangle can make 15 tarts.
Text 4	The division of fractions algorithm is $a/b \div c/d = a/b \times d/c$ that is: a/b divided by c/d is equal to a/b multiplied by the reciprocal of c/d. In this case: $10 \div 2/3 = 10 \times 3/2$ $10 \times 3 = 30$ $30 \div 2 = 15$

Table 3.1 Example 'texts' that students encounter as they learn mathematics

1 Which of the following contexts does each 'text' correspond to? How do you know?
   A From a student's written explanation of how to solve the problem
   B From a student's textbook
   C Spoken by a small group of students with accompanying action or gesture
   D Spoken by a student about the action, after the event
2 In what order would you engage your students in these activities? Why?

These 'texts' illustrate how language shifts as children move from more interactional contexts to more academic contexts in which they speak formally, read, and write.

Text 1 corresponds to Context C: it's spoken by a small group of students with accompanying action or gesture. We know this because of the language that is being used: commands ('mark', 'try') and other interactional language ('no', 'OK').

Text 2 corresponds to Context D: it's spoken by a student about the action, after the event. Here, the student uses past tense verbs ('drew', 'cut', 'counted') and sequencing and consequence conjunctions ('then', 'so') to report on what the group did.

Text 3 corresponds to Context A: it's a student's written explanation of how to solve the problem. It uses present tense verbs ('want to find', 'can divide', 'count') to make statements that are general and timeless. It draws on conjunctions that present the conditions under which the different processes occur ('when', 'since'). It also uses a reference term, 'That', to help the writer draw a conclusion ('That means … ').

Text 4 corresponds to Context B: it's a passage from the students' textbook. It draws on language features typical of written academic language such as long noun phrases ('the division of fractions algorithm') and technical vocabulary from the subject area ('divided', 'multiplied', 'reciprocal').

We see the functionality of the grammatical choices used here to accomplish the different goals of the texts and activities. Recognizing the functionality of the language resources helps you decide what grammar to focus on in order to enable students to participate in these different kinds of tasks and engage with different texts.

The way you sequence instructional activities can help your students build from the language they may be more familiar with into more unfamiliar forms. Teachers often begin a unit of instruction with concrete, hands-on activities, and we can see here that doing so helps students draw on the interactional language with which they are likely more comfortable. Having students report on what they have done in small groups gives them practice in retelling, a common activity in the primary school curriculum, and as they do so, the teacher can focus their attention on the past tense verbs that they need for this task, along with the sequencing connectors. We saw in Chapter 2 how Doughty and Varela found that a focus on the particular language forms needed for science reports helped students develop the ability to report on what they had learned in their science class. Next, in supporting students to construct a written explanation about how to solve the problem, the teacher can talk about the present tense and why we use it to write or talk about something timeless or general. Students can look at how 'when' and 'since' introduce conditions in the explanation, and might practice writing sentences using these conjunctions. In reading about division of fractions in the textbook, the teacher might work with the students to deconstruct the long noun groups, examining what the parts mean and how they go together. Teachers might even choose to start with the abstract textbook language and then move students to the more concrete, hands-on activity. In each case, building in talk about language through metalanguage that names the language in focus helps the children learn grammar while they learn mathematics.

In this chapter, we present studies that show how teachers can support primary students' L2 learning through talk in the classroom, reading and noticing language forms and their functions in curriculum materials, and writing using new forms appropriate for specific writing tasks. The goal of this chapter is to raise your awareness about differences in the grammar of texts from varied subject areas. This will prepare you to choose a grammar teaching focus that addresses your particular curricular objectives. In the next section, we discuss learning grammar through talk.

Learning Grammar through Talk in Primary School

As we saw in Chapter 2, the role of classroom talk for L2 learners' language development has been well established in the research literature (Gibbons, 2002; see also Wells, 1994, 1999). Language production is key to supporting learning a second language (Swain, 1995); interaction enables L2 learners to use the grammatical resources they have but also come to know and use new ones. The development of oral language is crucial for children's language development in general and is the basis on which learners move toward greater second language proficiency. L2 learners need opportunities to participate in talk in the context of meaningful classroom activities that enable them to meet the increasing demands of the subject areas (see Oliver

& Philp, 2014). Children can build their knowledge about language through talk about how language works in presenting academic content. This needs to be a significant part of classroom activities: oral interaction that takes place around texts is essential for students as a bridge between their everyday language and their learning of disciplinary language (Gibbons, 1998, 2003, 2006a, 2006b).

Teachers play a major role in developing children's oral language ability by elaborating on their production, recasting their contributions into more appropriate wording, giving them access to different grammatical patterns in the discourse, and promoting reformulation of their expressions (Gibbons, 2006a). These are the activities identified by Gibbons' four pedagogical moves described in Chapter 2. You will use them to analyze examples of classroom interaction presented in the research reported in this chapter.

L2 learners also need opportunities to talk about language itself. Talking about language requires metalanguage that makes meaningful connections between the forms language takes and the purposes for learning. Using a metalanguage helps teachers to make grammar more visible in meaningful activities which support literacy and subject-matter learning. The use of metalanguage is more than just naming a particular grammatical feature: it means drawing L2 learners' attention to how the language functions, enabling a discussion about ideas in the texts they read and are expected to write. Metalanguage assists teachers in raising students' consciousness about grammar and grammatical structure so students can both recognize and draw on those structures in their own speaking and writing.

In Chapter 1, we presented a classroom snapshot of a primary school teacher working with her students to help them recognize that different speech functions in English (statement, question, offer, command) are accomplished through three grammatical mood options (declarative, interrogative, imperative) and to consider the effect of those choices on the listener in the context of reading a story. The story has lots of safety tips from a police officer who visits schools, and these are presented as commands about what to do. The class analyzes these, deciding what mood the author has chosen to give a command.

In Classroom Snapshot 1.1, the teacher uses talk to build L2 learners' knowledge about the language used to express a command. In this context, 'command' is functional, meaning-focused metalanguage. The teacher shows students how the grammar that presents commands can be either declarative, interrogative, or imperative, and the children classify the commands into these three grammatical patterns. Table 3.2 shows how some of the commands the children analyzed were expressed during the conversation and in the story.

Speech function/ grammatical mood	Declarative	Interrogative	Imperative
Command	'I'd like someone to close the door.'	'Can you give me a command?' 'Would you please sit right?'	'Keep your shoelaces tied.' 'Always wipe up spills before someone slips and falls.'

Table 3.2 Speech function/grammatical mood (adapted from Schleppegrell, 2013)

The students learn grammar as they participate in a meaningful classroom activity. The teacher's question—'Hussein, do you know a command, can you give me a command?'—and Hussein's answer—'Well, you just said one'—prompt an exchange about how commands are expressed in English. In the discussion with students that follows, the teacher asks them whether they think she gave them a command. Some students answer 'yes' and others 'no', and yet by the end of the exchange, when the teacher asks 'What kind of a command?' and students answer 'A question', the teacher responds 'I'm interrogating', and they all agree that she gave them a command in the form of a question (Schleppegrell, 2013, p. 159).

Look again at Classroom Snapshot 1.1 (see page 4) as you do Activity 3.2.

Activity 3.2

Think about Gibbons' pedagogical moves (1 'talking about language, using meaningful metalanguage'; 2 'unpacking written language'; 3 'recasting student discourse'; 4 'reminding and handing over'). Which are exemplified in Classroom Snapshot 1.1? Refer to the detailed explanation of these moves that we have provided in Chapter 2. What does the teacher accomplish through those moves?

In terms of Gibbons' mode-shifting moves, we see that the teacher engages students in two ways: by being explicit in talk about language using metalanguage that is made meaningful (Gibbons' first pedagogical move) and by unpacking written language (the second move). The activity itself is meaningful for the children because they are talking about the story they are reading. This talk about different kinds of commands helps them think about what makes a command 'polite', who gets to command someone else and how, and other issues related to **sociolinguistic competence**. They also write commands using the grammar they have been focusing on.

Gibbons (2006a) illustrated movement between more everyday and more formal ways of expression in a science classroom. She showed how teachers planned their activities to move from classroom talk to writing over a unit of instruction, with talk about grammar built into the pedagogy at each stage. Spotlight Study 3.1 reports on how this planning supported a focus on the science content to be learned but also drew students' attention to language they could use to more authoritatively present that content. The teacher gave students feedback on their language choices while they spoke and wrote, thus moving them back and forth along the mode continuum.

Spotlight Study 3.1

Gibbons (2006a) investigated how science classroom discourse enabled linguistically and culturally diverse elementary students to move from everyday ways of making meaning toward more technical, subject-specific forms of expression for talking and writing about science. In the two fifth grade science classrooms Gibbons studied in Australia, 92 percent of the students were L2 learners of English. Most appeared fluent in conversational English but were less familiar with the content-specific ways that language is used in school science. The unit topic was magnetism. One activity consisted of four experiments designed to develop students' understanding of magnetic attraction and repulsion. Teachers planned classroom talk through three-stage classroom activities. These involved:

1 group-talking: doing a hands-on experiment in small groups
2 teacher-guided reporting: recounting the actions and outcomes of the hands-on experiment to the whole class
3 written reports: completing writing tasks in science journals.

Gibbons analyzed the spoken interactions in the classroom and students' written texts to identify how the teachers provided linguistic support for ELLs in talking about what was being learned in both everyday and academic English. ■

Classroom Snapshot 3.1 shows how the teacher uses what Gibbons calls 'bridging discourse', bringing together 'everyday and subject-specific ways of meaning, thus building on students' prior knowledge and current language as a way of introducing them to new language' (Gibbons, 2009, p. 62). It provides an example of how the teacher's talk moved back and forth from less formal to more 'scientific' language as she co-constructed with students their oral reports on their hands-on group-work with magnets. This talk about magnetism then served as preparation for writing in more technical ways. Gibbons represents the teacher's talk in two columns to show how she moves back and forth between everyday and more technical language.

Classroom Snapshot 3.1

Student	Teacher	
	(Everyday)	(Formal)
it *sticks* together		
	like that (demonstrating)	
		they *attracted* to each other
you can feel … that they're not pushing … if we use the other side we can't feel *pushing*	they *stuck* to each other	
		when they were facing one way you felt the magnets *attract*
	and *stick* together	
		when you turn one of the magnets around you felt it *repelling*
	or *pushing* away	

Table 3.3 A teacher's use of 'bridging discourse' (adapted from Gibbons, 2006a)

We noted in Chapter 2 that the use of the term *recast* in Gibbons' framework is somewhat different from its use in the focus on form studies reported there. In those studies, the role of teacher recasts was to model correct forms, reformulating students' utterances to make them more grammatically accurate. There, we learned that sometimes in meaning-focused discussion, primary-level students did not 'repair' their incorrect usage following a teacher recast (Lyster & Ranta, 1997). In Gibbons' framework, thinking about a recast as a modeling of more precise language that will eventually become part of the children's linguistic repertoires helps us see the value of this pedagogical move, even when it is not immediately taken up in the children's oral language. What this move does is give students access to alternative wording and grammatical patterns in authentic contexts where such patterns are functional. But the recasts don't occur in response to a student's error; instead, they are planned, regularly occurring restatements that model for students the language that the teacher wants to focus on throughout the unit of study. In the 'reminding and handing over' move, when students produce more formal oral or written reports of the experiments, they will be encouraged to use these more 'scientific' language patterns.

We see here how the teacher's recasts go beyond feedback on accuracy to show students how the meanings they are presenting can be reformulated in the more technical ways valued in science. The teacher recasts 'magnets stick' and 'not pushing' into 'magnets attract' and 'repelling' (p. 130). Gibbons points out that the teacher, in her recast, is expressing the same idea about magnets as the student, shown in the different words used to represent the same scientific content: 'stick'/'attract'; 'not pushing'/'repelling'. As the teacher develops and repeats the same scientific content, she continually shifts back and forth between everyday and scientific language: 'they stuck to each other'/'they attracted to each other'; 'when you turn one of the magnets around you felt it repelling'/'or pushing away' (p. 130). This shifting uses students' everyday language as a resource to bridge to more scientific language. We position this practice of saying the same thing in different ways as grammar teaching and this recasting as particularly important for L2 learners' language development, as they have few out-of-school opportunities to engage with technical language needed for talking and writing about school subjects. While this activity also helps students learn new vocabulary, it is primarily an exercise in expanding their grammatical resources to help them speak and write about the science they are learning. Students are practicing talking as scientists would talk about magnetism. ■

For Gibbons, the four pedagogical moves are always part of the ongoing dialogue in the classroom as it unfolds over a unit of instruction. Therefore, these recasts occur in contexts where the teacher consistently uses metatalk that reminds students about using more scientific language (first pedagogical move: 'talking about language, using meaningful metalanguage'). The teacher also repeatedly engages in working with students to unpack the written language that is scientific (second pedagogical move: 'unpacking written language'). Through the recasts (third pedagogical move), the teacher moves back and forth between saying the magnets 'attract' and 'stick together', 'repel' and 'push away', modeling how the technical and everyday terms relate to each other. The recast moves occur throughout the unit and, by the end, the teacher is reminding students about the academic language needed to express themselves and expecting them to use it themselves (fourth pedagogical move: 'reminding and handing over').

The 'reminding and handing over' is also done by asking students to write about what they have learned, enabling each of them to produce language that demonstrates their take-up of the new grammar. Gibbons (2006a) provides examples of the writing the children did before the discussion described in Classroom Snapshot 3.1 and then after the discussion, and of other work the teacher did to focus them on 'scientific' ways of talking and writing. One L2 learner, Julianne, wrote the following text before the discussion:

> The magnet which we put next didn't touch the other magnet. When we turned it over it stucked on the other.

(Gibbons, 2006a, p. 166)

This text is a recount of what the children did during the experiment, using 'we' and past tense verbs to retell what happened in a specific instance, and drawing on the everyday language *'stucked'. After the discussion, her text shifts to present information about magnetism, rather than about what the group had done. She writes about more general principles of magnetism, using the present tense and the generalized 'you' to describe what always holds true:

> All magnets have a side which repels and a side that attracts. Magnets don't stick if you put north with a north or south and a south but if you put a south with a north they stick.

(Gibbons, 2006a, pp. 166–7)

While she is still using some everyday vocabulary ('stick'), Julianne is now able to state a generalization about magnets using more sophisticated grammatical structures. She describes magnets and their features, and states general principles about them. She also represents conditional relationships in 'if' clauses and uses some of the scientific terminology the teacher helped her develop through recasts during the discussion.

'Reminding and handing over' was also done in oral language use throughout these activities, when the teacher thought the students were ready to draw on the new language without her modeling. For example, as a student is reporting on the work with magnets, following teacher modeling, she says, 'We found out that the south and the south don't like to stick together.' The teacher says, 'Now (…) let's start using our scientific language, Michelle.' With that prompt, the student says, 'The north and the north repelled each other and the south and the south also …' (Gibbons, 2006a, p. 138). This reminding prompts the student to notice her own language choices and recognize the inadequacy of her contribution in this context. By 'handing over' responsibility for the presentation of language in 'scientific' ways, the teacher enables the students to construct a grammatically more complete and appropriate presentation of scientific meaning.

Learning Grammar for Reading in Primary School

Teachers can also teach grammar in the context of helping students engage with the texts they read in primary schooling. We have seen in the mathematics and science examples above how language varies in the different kinds of activities we do. Another way language varies is in the different curriculum content areas. For example, language that presents emotions and attitudes will more often occur in narratives, while language that defines is likely to be more prominent in science texts. To be proactive in teaching grammar, teachers need to recognize how texts draw on different language forms to present different aspects of meaning. Choosing the grammar focus to support the content learning calls for an understanding of language patterns typical of different school subjects.

In Activity 3.3, you can explore differences between texts across content areas, paying attention to how these texts draw on different language forms to present different aspects of meaning.

Activity 3.3

Read the following history and science texts from a fourth grade classroom and identify some prominent language features. How do the texts differ in the grammatical choices the authors make, and why?

Text 1 (history)

Settling Alta California

Spain paid little attention to Alta California until the 1760s. Then King Carlos III of Spain heard that other countries, such as Russia, had started to explore the Pacific coast of North America. To protect Spanish claims, King Carlos ordered that settlements be built in Alta California.

The Spanish Return

King Carlos gave this order after he heard that Russia had set up a colony in Alaska. The King worried that Russian fur traders would move south from Alaska. They might try to set up a colony in California.

Starting a Spanish colony in Alta California was not easy, however. Travel to California was difficult, and few people wanted to move so far away. Spain decided that the best way to start a colony was to build missions, or religious settlements.

(Boehm et al., 2000, pp. 142–3)

Text 2 (science)

A cell is the building block of life. A cell is the smallest unit of a living thing that can perform all life processes. All living things are made of cells. Some living things are made up of just one cell. Most living things, like plants and animals, are many-celled. Every part of a cat—from its muscles to its blood—is made of thousands, millions, even billions of cells. Many cells have a particular role. Some cells help the living thing get energy it uses to grow, develop, and reproduce. Other cells help it get rid of what it doesn't need. Others help it to move or react to its environment. Still other cells may protect the living thing or help it stay healthy. All cells come only from other living cells.

(Scott Foresman Science, 2006, p. 7)

Use Table 3.4 as you compare these two texts. The questions in the first column will help you focus on important grammatical features of the two texts.

Grammatical choices	History text	Science text
How is time represented (verb tense, other expressions of time)?		
What kinds of circumstances and connectors are used?		
What kinds of processes are used (e.g. verbs of doing, thinking/feeling, saying, being)?		

Photocopiable © Oxford University Press

Table 3.4 Grammatical choices and history and science text analyses

The history text about settling Alta California uses past tense and circumstances and connectors that show time, such as 'until the 1760s', 'then', and 'after'. For example, consider the connector 'then' in 'Then King Carlos III of Spain heard that other countries, such as Russia, had started to explore the Pacific coast of North America'. This helps to construct a sequence of events by establishing a timeline. The text has mainly verbs of doing and thinking/feeling, as it is about events and the thinking and actions of King Carlos and the Spanish government. In the last paragraph, there are some being processes that describe travel as 'difficult' and starting a colony as 'not easy'. This is a text about what happened and why, and the grammatical choices of the author enable that purpose.

The science text uses mainly being processes to present definitions (for example, 'A cell is the smallest unit of a living thing that can perform all life processes') and describe the structure of cells. As there are no human participants in this text, there are no saying or thinking/feeling processes presented. In the last paragraph, a few doing processes report on what cells do in their functions. The main purpose of the text is to define and explain the roles of cells, and the grammar helps it do that.

The differences in the language used in these texts can be highlighted by teachers to show how these and other texts draw on different language forms to present different meanings. For example, a teacher might use the metalanguage of process type as students read the history text to help them recognize how a series of events is presented and how the King's thinking about those events is infused into the text. A focus on connectors and circumstances can help students see how time is presented in this text, thereby also accomplishing the lesson objective: to understand why missions were built in Alta California and the events that led to this. In teaching the science text, a teacher could focus on the grammar of being processes, exploring how 'is/are' and 'is made of/made up of' alternate to describe how cells make up living things. This can help teachers go beyond defining technical terms (for example, 'cell' and 'living things') to focus on patterns in the grammar that the students will also encounter in other texts they read. Students can examine the different parts of the text to see how cells are first defined in being processes and how their roles are then developed in doing processes. Thus students can begin to understand how defining/describing and explaining are done in science.

Metalanguage enables a purposeful focus on form and meaning through activities that provide appropriate contexts for introducing and using grammatical terms (Dare, 2010; de Oliveira, Lan, & Dodds, 2013; Moore & Schleppegrell, 2014). In Chapter 1, we saw some examples of metalanguage in use in primary Language Arts and secondary history classrooms. These examples of unit planning illustrated how after setting goals, motivating the learning, and engaging students with a 'text', teachers can use metalanguage to explore the language of the text. This provides a way of focusing on forms in a meaningful context.

In Activity 3.3, we used the metalanguage of process type to talk about typical differences in history and science texts. In Chapter 2, you learned that the functional grammar label *process* offers a way of identifying whole verb phrases as meaningful chunks. Recognizing different *types* of processes helps readers focus on the kinds of meanings that verbs present and think about how the nouns in the sentence/clause are related to the meaning in the verb.

This equips readers to look at a sentence and see *what is going on.* As children gain familiarity with functional labeling, they will come to expect that focusing on grammar will provide an understanding of how language works. They will come to see language in terms of meaning and social purpose.

Activity 3.4

Consider the sentences below from the history and science texts in Activity 3.3. Categorize each *italicized* process as presenting *doing, saying, sensing,* or *being.*

1 'Then King Carlos III of Spain *heard* that other countries, such as Russia, had started to explore the Pacific coast of North America.'
2 'The king *worried* that Russian fur traders would move south from Alaska.'
3 'To protect Spanish claims, King Carlos *ordered* that settlements be built in Alta California.'
4 'A cell *is* the building block of life.'
5 'Some cells *help* the living thing get energy it uses to grow, develop, and reproduce.'

'Heard' and 'worried' in 1 and 2 are sensing processes, reporting on what King Carlos perceived and felt. 'Order' in 3 is a saying process (whether in speaking or writing) that projects a doing process, the building of settlements. Sentence 4 presents a being process that defines a cell, and 5 a doing process that tells about the function of cells.

Drawing students' attention to the differences in process types and the kinds of structures they participate in can raise their consciousness about how English works. Using the metalanguage of process enables a focus on the whole meaningful unit without initially having to deal with the complications of verb group form in English (for example, students could identify 'was going to go' as a process without having to identify each separate constituent in that process as a particular kind of verb form). However, we recognize that this metalanguage may be unfamiliar. Teachers can accomplish similar goals by referring to these as *action (doing) verbs, saying verbs, thinking verbs,* and *being verbs.* We see this approach in Classroom Snapshot 3.2.

Classroom Snapshot 3.2

Bailey and Heritage (2008) discuss how a fifth grade teacher, Ms West, supports students' understanding of expository text in a social studies unit on America in the early nineteenth century. Students have just read a chapter that contained information about the Lewis and Clark expedition, part of the western exploration of the USA, and have taken notes on their reading. Ms West notices that one of the students in the classroom, Octavia, is not making a connection between the events in the text and the role of the rivers that Lewis and Clark explored. She decides to focus Octavia on a grammatical resource for making that connection by drawing her attention to the role of *action verbs* in the text and how they can help her understand the role of rivers in the expedition. The following presents the exchange between Ms West and Octavia.

Ms West: What did you think of the book, *The Incredible Journey of Lewis & Clark*?

Octavia: I didn't really like it that much.

Ms West: Oh no? How come?

Octavia: It was hard to tell what was going on.

    (…)

Ms West: (…) Do you have a sense of what these things you wrote about had to do with each other? For example, the expedition, the waterways, and the West?

Octavia: Not really.

Ms West: That's alright. I was thinking of a strategy that might help you. It's a strategy that readers of history often do to help them understand what they are reading. They pay special attention to the action verbs in the text. Do you remember what action verbs are?

Octavia: Yes, I remember. We had to find them in that chapter in *Island of the Blue Dolphins*.

Ms West: Exactly. Action verbs often can tell a reader what things and people do and how they are connected together. Let's take a quick look at the action verbs in the Lewis and Clark book and see if we can figure out how these ideas you wrote about in your reading log relate to one another. [Octavia opens book to the right pages.]

Octavia: Okay, here it is.

Ms West: Can you find the part where they talk about the expedition and the waterways?

Octavia: It's right here. [Octavia points to the section in the text.]

Ms West: Great. Read to me some of the action verbs you find there.

Octavia: Cross, paddle, row, sail …

Ms West: Great. Do these words give you any hint about what the waterways had to do with the expedition?

Octavia: Well, maybe they had to get beyond them, to cross them in the expedition.

Ms West: I think so too! Very good. I think you may have a strategy that can work for you.

(Bailey & Heritage, 2008, pp. 142–4)

In order to recognize how the rivers played a role in the expedition, Ms West asks Octavia to find the action verbs: 'cross', 'paddle', 'row', 'sail'. This is not talk about verbs in general, but instead focuses Octavia on the meaning that a particular set of verbs—action verbs—plays in developing the challenges and affordances rivers posed in exploration of the West. Ms West refers to this as a reading 'strategy' that Octavia can use when she reads other history texts. As Ms West says, 'Action verbs often can tell a reader what things and people do and how they are connected together', and this is a common focus in discussing events in history.

But in addition to being a reading strategy, this is also grammar teaching, as it draws attention to form–meaning relationships. In this particular case, a focus on action verbs can contribute to students' understanding about language, as it helps them recognize that verbs do not always present actions. Verbs are sometimes casually defined by teachers as 'action words', a misleading way of helping students understand the role of different kinds of verbs in constructing meaning in texts of different types. ■

In reading texts across subject areas, teachers and students can focus on language and unpack written text to explore the ways the grammar is used to construct different meanings. De Oliveira and Dodds (2010) show the application of this approach in science lessons designed for L2 students at intermediate to advanced levels of language proficiency in mainstream classrooms. Activity 3.5 shows how the teacher uses functional grammar metalanguage to engage students in talk about science and address some language challenges of reading science texts. The main goal is to discuss the scientific meanings and help students learn to recognize patterns in the grammar through which those meanings are presented in text.

Activity 3.5

De Oliveira and Dodds (2010) suggest how grammatical metalanguage can be introduced to support productive conversations about language and meaning. This activity is adapted from that work.

Katie Dodds developed language-based science lessons to help her fourth grade English language learners at various levels of English language proficiency read the difficult textbook they were working with. In this lesson, the students are revisiting a text they read the day before in order to become more familiar with the content as they focus on the language. This is the paragraph the class is reading:

Jupiter

Jupiter, the fifth planet from the Sun, is a gas giant. A gas giant is a very large planet made mostly of gases. Jupiter's atmosphere is mainly hydrogen and helium. Jupiter is the largest planet in our solar system. In fact, if it were hollow, it is so big that all of the other planets could fit inside of it!

(Scott Foresman Science, 2006, p. 528)

The teacher's goal is to help the students unpack this written text to look for patterns and learn how to read the text closely to understand the ideas being presented. She models this process by co-constructing the analysis of the first sentence in the text and then asks the students to work in pairs to complete the chart below. The students are familiar with the metalanguage of process type, participant, and connector. In previous lessons, the teacher had introduced the notion of different types of processes, participants, and connectors, and had displayed definitions on the classroom wall. For this particular lesson, she had posted the following information:

Participant: The main participant is the whole noun group that is the subject
Being Process: Verbs that help us define and describe
Connector: A word or words that tell us how different processes are related

The teacher asks: 'What is the process in the first sentence? What are the two participants in that process?' The students recognize that the main participant occurs before the being process 'is' and that what comes after the process is how the main participant is defined or described. Then they work together to complete the rest of the chart, analyzing the other sentences in the paragraph. You try it!

Connector	Main participant	Process	How the main participant is defined or described
	Jupiter, the fifth planet from the Sun,	is	a gas giant.

Photocopiable © Oxford University Press

Table 3.5 Text analysis using the metalanguage of process type, participant, and connector

After the students work together in pairs to fill in the chart, they complete it at the front of the room with their analysis. Here's how it looked:

Connector	Main participant	Process	How the main participant is defined or described
	Jupiter, the fifth planet from the Sun,	is	a gas giant.
	A gas giant	is	a very large planet made mostly of gases.
	Jupiter's atmosphere	is	mainly hydrogen and helium.
	Jupiter	is	the largest planet in our solar system.
In fact, if	it	were	hollow,
	it	is	so big that all of the other planets could fit inside of it!

Table 3.6 Completed text analysis using the metalanguage of process type, participant, and connector

The class discusses the different ways the main participant in the text, Jupiter, is referred to: as a 'gas giant', with the pronoun 'it', and with reference to its 'atmosphere'. The students see that all of the processes here are being processes. The discussion then focuses on the Main Participant column, as this often contains the most challenging scientific information. In some cases, this may need to be further examined to explore how the meanings are presented. The students see all the ways Jupiter is described: as 'a very large planet made mostly of gases', 'mainly hydrogen and helium', and as 'the largest planet in our solar system'. They recognize that the connector 'In fact, if' sets up a condition that is not real (as Jupiter is not hollow) followed by a statement about how big Jupiter is.

Once the teacher is confident that the students understand the text, she gives them some questions to promote discussion. She has developed these questions to build from the grammar analysis and relate the scientific content of the text to students' prior knowledge about the solar system:

- What do you imagine when you hear the words 'a gas giant'?
- Is Jupiter's atmosphere similar to Earth's?
- What other planets are in our solar system?
- What 'other planets' does the author refer to?

The questions are a reminder to focus on both the language and the science being expressed through the language. In creating the lesson, the focus was on the content to be learned and the key questions to be answered at the end. The unpacking of the written text supported the students in answering those questions.

The notion of process type is also useful for students as they read narrative texts. They can identify a character's actions by finding doing processes, or identify characters' feelings by identifying sensing or being processes. Exploring a character's engagement in those processes can help students understand the character and the character's development over the course of a story.

Spotlight Study 3.2

Moore and Schleppegrell (2014) show how teachers use the metalanguage of process type to support Language Arts activities focused on characters' feelings. They describe how students looked at the different ways characters' feelings are represented in a story, identifying the kind of process the author uses to present the feelings and the strength of those feelings. For example, 'He was kind of disappointed' represents a somewhat negative feeling presented in a being process. 'She jumped for joy' represents an enthusiastic positive feeling presented in a doing process. Using this metalanguage, students were able to see how authors often use doing or saying processes, and not just sensing and being processes, to show how characters feel. Since the doing and saying processes are not direct statements about feelings, they need to be interpreted. For example, '"Stay away," he growled' requires reading 'growled' as expressing negative feelings. Teachers encouraged students to think about the feelings implied in doing and saying processes, and to restate them more explicitly as sensing or being processes. For example, students would read the sentence 'She slumped down in her chair' and rewrite it as 'She was disappointed'. This engages students in the kind of interpretation they need to do to talk and write about characters and their development.

Doing this work involved lots of discussion about meaning in the context of reading and interpretation of the text. It also supported vocabulary development, as the English language learners in the study often had few adjectives other than 'happy' or 'sad' to describe the feelings they were interpreting. Developing ways to express more complex meanings led to the introduction of new vocabulary in meaningful contexts; this vocabulary then served as a resource for the children when they wrote about the characters they were analyzing and discussing. For example, Moore and Schleppegrell (2014) report that when the story said a character 'felt anxious', the students did not initially understand what 'anxious' would mean in that context, where the character was worried. Most of them knew the word only in its everyday meaning of 'excited'—anxious for a holiday to come, for example. The activities described here illustrate how discussion about the language of a text enables children to recast what an author has written in more informal, everyday language, revealing misunderstandings. At the same time, this discussion also focuses students on what the author achieves through the use of more literary or technical language.

This helps to develop students' linguistic repertoires and expand their lexical and grammatical resources for meaning-making.

This conversation about text and use of grammatical metalanguage also enables the teacher to move the talk along the mode continuum, as the students identify feelings expressed in literary language. Moore and Schleppegrell report on how the metalanguage of process type and the interpretation of feelings helped students identify the ways authors use language for character development by presenting characters' attitudes in implicit and explicit ways. The researchers suggest that this use of functional metalanguage offers new ways for teachers to support ELLs' development of academic language, while simultaneously engaging them in challenging curricular tasks. ■

Activity 3.6

The following sentences come from *Officer Buckle and Gloria*, the story featured in Classroom Snapshot 1.1 (see page 4). Underline the words in these sentences that show feelings. What feeling is shown or told? Then identify the process types through which the feelings are presented. What does this help you see about how the language is being used?

Before Gloria, the dog, starts coming along with Officer Buckle:

Officer Buckle shared his safety tips with the students at Napville School. Nobody ever listened.
Sometimes, there was snoring.

After Gloria starts coming along:

Officer Buckle gave Safety Tip Number One:
'KEEP your SHOELACES tied!' The children sat up and stared.
(…)
Officer Buckle thought of a safety tip he had discovered that morning.
(…)
'NEVER leave a THUMBTACK where you might SIT on it!'
The audience roared.

Officer Buckle grinned. He said the rest of the tips with *plenty* of expression. The children clapped their hands and cheered. Some of them laughed until they cried.

(Rathmann, 1995, no page numbers)

Did you identify these processes as representing feelings?

- 'Nobody ever listened. Sometimes, there was snoring.' (the children were bored; doing processes)
- 'The children sat up and stared.' (they are getting interested; doing processes)
- 'The audience roared.' (they are very excited; doing/saying process)
- 'Officer Buckle grinned.' (he is happy; doing process)
- 'The children clapped their hands and cheered. Some of them laughed until they cried.' (they are very excited and happy; doing processes)

We can see how the author presents the characters' feelings through their *doing*. Initially, the children's behavior shows that they are bored by the lectures ('nobody ever listened'; 'there was snoring'). After Officer Buckle brings the dog Gloria along, the atmosphere changes dramatically. Again, the author uses the children's doing to show the reader how they feel. Discussion about the meaning of these sentences, why the author has made these language choices, and how feeling can be presented in doing helps the children see how the resources of English can be drawn on to *show*, not *tell*, how a character feels. This supports the goals of the Language Arts class as well as helping students focus on the varied ways feelings can be represented in language.

Analyzing the *doing* processes and reinterpreting their meanings as feelings in *being* processes helps readers see that feelings can be expressed either directly in being or sensing processes or indirectly in doing processes. Identifying and categorizing these different ways of presenting feelings helps learners make sense of the characters' feelings even when they are conveyed through actions, and the talk about text helps them identify meaningful grammatical segments in the text and how they work together. This noticing of how the language works puts a focus on grammar and meaning simultaneously. It supports talk about text that enhances students' opportunities to engage deeply with the meaning while also learning about how those meanings can be expressed.

Learning Grammar for Writing in Primary School

After talking about language, using meaningful metalanguage, deconstructing text, and moving along the mode continuum through recasts, teachers should engage in the pedagogical move of reminding and handing over. This occurs after the students have built up metalinguistic knowledge and can also serve as a means of assessing students' learning. Writing instruction is a powerful context for addressing grammar, but to realize its potential for supporting grammatical development, teachers need to go beyond correcting students' errors and understand the kinds of language choices that are relevant to accomplishing specific types of writing tasks. They should also think of the types of text, or genres, to be written and what is important in each genre—its purpose and language features (see Rose & Martin, 2012, for a discussion of genres). Research that illustrates this point is reported in Spotlight Study 3.3. This shows how a teacher guided students to write in a particular genre, helping them to use the appropriate text features and gain greater control of the academic register needed to perform the writing task effectively.

Spotlight Study 3.3

Gebhard, Harman, and Seger (2007) describe how a fifth grade teacher, Wendy, uses a focus on grammar to help her L2 learners use academic language to write arguments. Her students had responded to a previous writing assignment by using informal and oral-like linguistic strategies to form arguments, writing, for example: 'That is not fair that students (…) CAN NOT HAVE RECESS!!!!!!!!!' (p. 423). Wendy decided to help them learn how to argue more authoritatively and persuasively, using register features that are more valued in English Language Arts. This was not an issue of grammatical correctness, but one of grammatical choices that fit better with the register of academic writing. Informed by systemic functional linguistics, Wendy developed mini-lessons using texts that modeled grammatical structures appropriate for arguing in more measured ways, and drew students' attention to how to use those structures effectively. Students worked along the mode continuum, collaborating in talking about their plans for writing and giving each other advice. The teacher provided feedback showing how words, sentence patterns, and organizational structures work in the kind of persuasive writing she wanted them to practice. The assignment was to write a letter to their principal, challenging school policies regarding recess that had upset the children.

In one mini-lesson, Wendy showed her students the organizational structure of a sample letter. She highlighted how it used specific conjunctions such as 'although' and 'therefore' and types of sentence structures such as 'if/then' clauses to make its arguments stronger by conceding points of agreement, drawing conclusions, and setting up conditions. The students completed several mini-lessons and analyzed some key grammatical features of a text about the value of recess for students' academic growth. The teacher then asked them to draw on their notes on that text and the argument models posted on the classroom wall to write a draft of their own persuasive letters to the principal. The article presents a case study of Julia, a student who used the grammatical and structural features introduced by Wendy to write more effectively. Gebhard et al. report that in Julia's final text 'the structure of her letter reflects the linguistic features

Wendy explicitly taught: it has an opening statement, a thesis, arguments, evaluation, and a concluding request, but it also retains the strong message that Julia established in her first free-write' (p. 426). In her final text, Julia uses more authoritative structures to send her message, writing, for example: 'Students learn better when they have a break. If you want us to learn better, then please consider giving us a break' (p. 427). She drew on a variety of conjunctions (for example, 'since', 'when', 'until', and 'but') to create coherence in the text and to develop her ideas in terms of time and condition. ■

Spotlight Study 3.3 highlights the importance of a proactive focus on grammar in the context of writing instruction. The teacher raised students' awareness of grammatical choices that fit better with the type of academic writing they had to produce. This was not primarily an issue of grammatical correctness, but instead of grammar as meaning-making. In the end, Julia produced a letter that drew on the linguistic features the teacher had explicitly taught, adopting the particular genre expectations of a persuasive text, using more authoritative structures, and structuring the text for overall **coherence** and **cohesion**.

Genre and effective and appropriate language features for that genre are also in focus in Activity 3.7, this time in a writing lesson in science.

Activity 3.7

De Oliveira and Lan (2014) describe a collaboration with a fourth grade mainstream teacher, 'Mrs Darcy' (a pseudonym), to develop support for her diverse students, who were learning to write about experiments relating to the science topic of density. Following their exploration of density in classroom interaction and experimentation, students were supported in writing a genre that reports on such experiments, the *procedural recount*. The researchers identified ways that a genre-based pedagogy informed by functional grammar could enhance Mrs Darcy's teaching of procedural recounts, with an explicit focus on the language of this genre.

Table 3.7 displays the purpose, text structure, and grammatical features typical of the procedural recount genre. The components of a procedural recount include the *Materials*, in which the writer records the materials or equipment that was used; the *Aim*, in which the writer states the purpose of the experiment; the *Record of Events*, in which the writer reports what was done in a sequenced way; and the *Conclusion*, in which the writer presents the outcome of the experiment. Table 3.8 provides a model of such a text.

Genre	Procedural recount
Purpose	To recount in order and with precision; a procedural recount records the materials, aims, steps, results, and conclusion of a scientific activity already conducted.
Text structure	• Materials • Aim • Record (what we did, what we observed) • Conclusion
Grammatical features	• Declarative sentences • Use of first person pronouns to retell the events • Doing processes • Past tense • Sequence connectors

Table 3.7 Genre, purpose, text structure, and grammatical features

Materials required	*2 pill bottles (one with a cap)* *50 beans* *Water*
Aim	*To demonstrate that plants need air*
Record (what we did/what we observed)	What we did: *First we soaked 50 beans. Then we filled both bottles with the soaked beans and put a little water in the bottom of each. Next we put the cap tight on one of the bottles and left the other open. Finally we shook the water over the beans.* What we observed: *The seeds [in the bottle with the cap off] started to sprout.*
Conclusion	*Plants need air to grow.*

Table 3.8 Example of a procedural recount (adapted from Christie & Derewianka, 2010, p. 155)

De Oliveira and Lan provide examples written by an ELL, Ji Soo, that show changes in his writing after the genre work. Here is the first text created by Ji Soo, before the genre work:

> When the soap thingy got mixed with the corn syrup, the soap turned kind of green. Then when I mixed it with red water, it turned kind of blue again. Then when we mixed with corn oil, pink bubbles formed between the corn oil and red water.

(de Oliveira & Lan, 2014, p. 32)

The teacher recognized that Ji Soo and other students needed support in structuring their reports on the experiment, and she also saw that they needed a focus on the kind of scientific language that they could use to present their results in more authoritative ways. Can you identify some language choices Ji Soo makes that could be improved upon to help him write a more scientific report?

The teacher used the model text to help students understand how to structure their texts, using the four stages of a procedural recount. She placed particular emphasis on the language features the model text used in the Record stage to recount events in order and with more precision. These features included the grammar of connectors and vocabulary choices such as the technical terms needed to name specific experimental materials. The teacher highlighted these features in the model text's Record stage and talked about why they were effective choices for writing about experiments. The teacher and students then did another experiment and wrote about it. The following text is what Ji Soo produced after the genre work and the second experiment. What are some key differences in the language that Ji Soo uses in this text?

Materials:
- styrofoam ball
- rubber band
- paper clip
- cup
- corn oil
- red water
- dishwater soap
- corn syrup

Aim:

To find the density.

Record:

First we poured corn syrup. Then we poured dishwater soap and it made 2 layers. Then we poured red water on the dishwater soap and it mixed a little bit. Finally we poured corn oil. Then we put a styrofoam ball, a paper clip, and a rubber band. We thought the ball will float, the paper clip will be in the middle, and the rubber band will float.

Conclusion:

The ball floated, and the paper clip and the rubber band sank to the bottom.

(de Oliveira & Lan, 2014, p. 36)

A close look at Ji Soo's texts produced before and after the instruction reveals that he was better able to use the language of procedural recounts following the genre-based work. Like Wendy, the teacher from Gebhard et al.'s study, Mrs Darcy explicitly talked about the language of the model text. She brought specific attention to the way the writer recorded events in order using sequencing connectors, and with precision using the correct terms to name the experimental materials.

Ji Soo's writing after the genre work reflects his increasing ability to record events with precision and in order, his greater control of field-specific vocabulary in naming materials, and his use of sequencing connectors. Ji Soo refers to the liquid as 'dishwater soap', revising his previous, more colloquial choice 'the soap thingy'. He expands his use of technical processes beyond the 'poured' he used in the first text, with 'mixed', 'put', 'floated', and 'sank'. The teacher's deconstruction of and explicit talk about the language of the model text strengthened Ji Soo's ability to link his ideas by using the sequencing connectors 'first', 'then', and 'finally', and to record events in order, rather than repeatedly using 'then' and 'when'.

Summary

In this chapter, we have reviewed research that offers new ways of understanding how grammar instruction in the primary grades can support L2 development by expanding L2 learners' grammatical resources to accomplish subject-specific tasks. We have shown how movement along the mode continuum enables teachers to draw on the oral language that L2 learners may already have developed and build on that through explicit attention to language form and meaning in the context of classroom interaction, deconstruction of written texts, and support for writing. Across a unit of study, students can be engaged in exploratory talk with peers, reporting on that talk, exploration of written text, and preparation for writing that helps them notice and use new language choices. By using grammatical metalanguage to deconstruct written text and explore meaning, teachers can help students make sense of academic language and identify how particular language choices are used for particular purposes.

We have also illustrated the use of Gibbons' four mode-shifting moves to engage students in noticing and using new language forms. Through talk about language, the teacher makes the noticing explicit and focused. By unpacking written language, using meaningful metalanguage, teachers equip learners to recognize meaningful grammatical segments in texts and how they work together. By modeling appropriate language choices through recasts, teachers keep the language forms in focus while supporting content learning and appropriate levels of academic and technical language use. And in reminding and handing over, teachers can plan instruction to move from classroom talk to writing and keep the focus on content as L2 learners discover useful language for presenting that content more authoritatively. A proactive focus on grammar supports talk for learning about language, talk for engagement with texts, and writing development, and helps move students into greater control of academic registers.

In addition, we have introduced ways of supporting students' exploration and use of these grammatical features:

- *mood and speech function* to identify who is commanding, asking, stating, and offering, and how they are engaging in those speech functions
- *circumstances and connectors* to contrast texts in different subject areas
- *verb tense* and how it varies when we use language for different purposes
- *processes of different types* (*doing, saying, sensing,* and *being*) to examine differences across subject areas, what is going on in a text, and how an author is presenting feelings and actions
- *participants* to explore how meaning is built up across a text as participants are defined and developed
- *connectors* to recognize how clauses are linked and how information flows in a text, bringing coherence through appropriate selection of logical meaning.

In discussing how these grammatical features can be highlighted, we have shown how the subject area, task, and genre are relevant to supporting effective language choices. We have illustrated how exploration of genre and text structure can be linked with a focus on grammar to prepare students for writing in more effective ways. We have also shown how grammar instruction can promote more effective language choices for accomplishing the tasks of schooling, rather than just grammatical accuracy and correctness.

To support primary school students in developing literacy and oral language skills across the required range of genres, teachers can help them see how language works to make meaning. Learning to talk, read, and write involves the development of grammar, and the primary school classroom is an important context for engaging in the mode-shifting described in this chapter and in Chapter 2. Children can build from their everyday language toward more abstract and distanced meanings that call for new ways of drawing on the grammatical systems of the language. In the early primary grades, all students begin to develop literacy and continue to develop their oral language skills for new kinds of tasks related to the learning goals of school. As they move into secondary school, they will be better prepared to engage with the more dense, abstract, and technical language that they will encounter there. Chapter 4 suggests how teachers in the secondary school can continue to provide support for grammar learning in the context of learning school subjects, as simultaneous focus on form and meaning continues to help learners develop complexity in their expression of meaning.

4

Classroom-Based Research on Grammar: Adolescent Learners

Preview

In this chapter, we will explore how grammar has been taught in meaningful ways to students aged 12–18 years. We will see how the learning opportunities and academic demands for secondary school students are different from those of the younger learners we read about in Chapter 3. We will link the classroom research to the theory and research presented in Chapter 2, including Gibbons' pedagogical moves and the notion of the mode continuum.

What Do Students Need to Learn about Grammar in Secondary School?

The theory of teaching and learning L2 grammar developed in Chapter 2 established that explicit attention to grammar facilitates L2 learning, but that grammar needs to be taught in meaningful contexts. We also pointed out that noticing and selective attending are key mechanisms that support L2 development. The theories of language discussed in that chapter—that L2 grammar emerges in social interaction, Halliday's perspective on register variation, and Gibbons' notion of the mode continuum—highlighted the variability in language that learners encounter as they move toward proficiency. All of this suggests that teachers need to help learners notice grammatical forms and recognize their roles in meaning-making. It also suggests that a focus on the expansion of the grammatical resources students control, rather than solely on accuracy in producing grammatical forms, is the best approach to grammar instruction for school-aged learners.

We have defined grammar as the full set of language resources through which meaning is presented, contrasting that view with the notion of grammar as a set of rules. Seeing grammar as a resource for meaning-making focuses attention on the patterns of language that students encounter across the years of schooling. In Chapter 3, we presented research that shows how teachers can support primary grade students' L2 learning through classroom activities that raise their awareness of the ways language is used in their curriculum materials and of how they can use new forms in their writing. We introduced some functional grammar metalanguage and demonstrated how it enables talk about grammar that also facilitates content learning across school subjects. In this chapter, we extend that focus, with a recognition that students in secondary school have increased developmental capacity for dealing with the abstraction of grammatical metalanguage and find the exploration of grammar to be an engaging, puzzle-like activity that is rewarding in the explicit insights about language form and use it helps them develop.

In the secondary school, the disciplinary demands increase along with the complexity of the grammatical forms students encounter. This chapter provides examples from research that has shown how teachers can engage students in talk about and exploration of grammar in the context of subject-area learning. These examples are presented to show how teachers can provide guidance in the grammatical choices students are expected to make in their writing. At this level, the construction of text and participation in discourse are crucial for secondary school students' engagement in the more advanced and technical learning required across subjects. The focus is on key grammatical structures that occur in the dense subject area texts of secondary school and that are needed for success in reading and writing academic registers. These include clause structures through which grammatical agency is presented, **nominalization** and **complex noun groups**, resources for conjunction and logical linking, and grammar that builds cohesion in text through effective reference. Research is presented that shows how teachers can draw explicit attention to these grammatical features while ensuring talk about grammar is also supportive of content learning. This is the direction that instruction needs to take for the L2 learner facing the challenge of learning school subjects and a second language simultaneously.

This chapter also presents research that illustrates how students in the secondary school years can engage in talk about grammar through which they explore form–meaning connections in the dense written language of the subject areas. This exploration encourages students to use different registers and to move back and forth in their language use across the mode continuum. It also enables development of the critical language awareness that teachers often consider a high priority in secondary school learning. The research suggests how to teach about grammar proactively, rather than just reacting to errors as a focus of grammar teaching. We will see that a focus on grammar can help with comprehension when reading, and with language production when writing, as well as support practice in speaking and listening.

As students move from primary to secondary school, they encounter difficult texts in every subject that use grammar in new, unfamiliar ways. As the knowledge they engage with becomes more technical and abstract, the grammar through which that knowledge is presented becomes likewise more dense, technical, and abstract. The grammatical patterns shift toward clauses that express relationships and present theoretical propositions, packing lots of information into each sentence. This is not just a question of learning new vocabulary; it is not just the choice of words that matters but also the choice of grammatical patterns. Subject-area texts are challenging to read in part because meanings are presented and developed in grammatical patterns that may be unfamiliar.

At the same time, the secondary school curriculum also requires that, increasingly, students respond in discipline-specific ways in writing across subjects. Teachers can support students' writing development by engaging in talk about what is expected and being explicit about the kinds of structures that will allow them to report, describe, explain, and argue in ways valued in disciplinary contexts.

As Chapters 1 and 2 established, a focus on grammar needs to serve other teaching goals as well. This chapter shows how grammar can be addressed while students are also engaging in rich discussions about the content of texts. The examples come from research in classrooms where the focus is most prominently on subject matter and where the talk about language is primarily in the service of disciplinary learning. In these examples, mainly from history and Language Arts classrooms, students look at the ways language is used in those disciplines to construct knowledge. We illustrate how talk about grammar can support the teacher's disciplinary goals.

Learning Grammar for Reading Secondary School Subjects

In this section, we review research that helps us understand how teachers can focus on grammar in the context of helping students read the challenging texts of secondary schooling. As we do so, we consider how the grammar students encountered in the primary years has evolved, bringing with it new challenges. As in Chapter 3, we show how teachers can be proactive about grammar teaching, using grammatical metalanguage and engaging students in movement across the mode continuum.

In Chapter 1, we presented a classroom snapshot of a teacher working with her students to explore historical agency in a middle school history classroom. The teacher was encouraging her students to look carefully at each clause of a multi-clause sentence to identify who the actors were and how they were presented in the grammar.

Activity 4.1

Look again at Classroom Snapshot 1.2 (see page 6) and then answer these questions.

1 Do you think this teacher's instructional practices focus on the key ideas presented so far in this chapter? Give examples of how you think the teacher is promoting disciplinary literacy and helping students learn about patterns in grammar relevant to learning history.
2 Which of Gibbons' pedagogical moves (1 'talking about language, using meaningful metalanguage'; 2 'unpacking written language'; 3 'recasting student discourse'; 4 'reminding and handing over') are exemplified in this snapshot? Refer to the detailed explanation of these moves in Chapter 2. Find examples of how you think the teacher is using the moves.

The teacher focuses on patterns in the presentation of agency that students may not be familiar with. In the sentence 'To finance Rome's huge armies, its citizens had to pay heavy taxes' (Frey, 2005, p. 8), the infinitive clause 'to finance … armies' identifies no explicit 'actor'/agent in the process 'to finance'. History discourse frequently uses infinitive clauses to introduce actions whose actors are not explicitly identified until the second clause. Participial clauses are often used in the same way, for example, 'Responding to Truman's plea, Congress approved $400 million in aid for Greece and Turkey' (Cayton, Perry, Reed, & Winkler, 2002, p. 490). To read sentences such as these with comprehension, students need to understand that the historical actors involved in the action in the initiating clause in each sentence will be identified in the following clause. By drawing attention to these grammatical patterns, the teacher helps students develop awareness about language–meaning connections that will support their comprehension of other history texts. In this case, the instruction is designed to focus students explicitly on the ways the author ascribes agency to the citizens of Rome with this infinitive clause (Schleppegrell et al., 2008). Teachers who recognize this challenge of history discourse can raise students' consciousness about the form–meaning connection, alerting them to texts where the initiating clause has no subject, and where they need to read on to identify who is responsible for the action.

In terms of Gibbons' mode-shifting moves, we see that the teacher engages students in two ways: by being explicit in talk about grammar and by using metalanguage that is made meaningful through the teacher's questions ('Who or what is doing the action presented in the verb? What does "its" refer to?'). Recall that metalanguage refers to both the terminology and the talk about language (Berry, 2005, 2010). Here, the talk about grammar also draws on the specific terms 'verb' and 'refer', both of which are part of the classroom discourse more generally as this teacher engages students in talk about text. The talk itself is a means of unpacking written language (Gibbons' second move) and helps students recognize how the language means what it does.

The students in Classroom Snapshot 1.2 are immigrant students who vary in language proficiency, many of them seemingly fluent in everyday English but still struggling with language tasks at school. The focus of the teacher is clearly on disciplinary literacy, as enabling students to recognize historical agency is a key goal of history teachers according to the California State History-Social Science Standards (California Department of Education, 2001). Identifying whom an author is presenting as responsible is not, however, always straightforward. This teacher is helping students recognize some specific ways English grammar is used to construct agency. Rather than doing this in decontextualized ways, the teacher is using a textbook passage, curriculum material that these English learners need to be able to work with, even though at present they find it very challenging. The complexity of the text is related to the complexity of the knowledge being presented and to the goals of instruction. Therefore, using such texts is important for engaging with students at their cognitive levels and supporting them in their learning of language and content simultaneously.

Snapshot 1.2 comes from a larger project where teachers were learning to talk about grammar with their students in support of learning both grammar and history. This larger project is the focus of Spotlight Study 4.1.

Spotlight Study 4.1

A series of articles shows how teachers in the California History Project (CHP) learned to talk about grammar in order to support ELLs in reading history. The CHP has provided professional development to improve history teachers' content knowledge and teaching skills since 1989. Beginning in 2000, the CHP, in collaboration with linguists at the University of California, Davis, developed specific approaches to address the needs of California's growing population of L2 learners, with particular attention to language issues involved in learning history.

A new program, Building Academic Literacy through History, was designed to support teachers in developing students' reading comprehension in history, critical perspectives toward texts, and academic writing. The CHP maintains partnerships with school districts to meet the needs of diverse student populations, with a focus on discipline-specific reasoning and preparing students to read and analyze text, use evidence, and write reasoned arguments. A key feature of the program is preparing teachers to lead discussion about the grammatical features of history texts in support of comprehension and development of strategies for reading independently. Teachers learn how to be proactive in their attention to grammar as they work with students to unpack the language of historical texts (de Oliveira, 2010, 2011, 2012; Schleppegrell & Achugar, 2003; Schleppegrell, Achugar, & Oteiza, 2004; Schleppegrell and de Oliveira, 2006; Schleppegrell et al., 2008). This process is described in Schleppegrell et al. (2004):

> … the teacher selects a passage from the textbook that has important history content related to the grade-level standards. Then the teacher leads the students in analyzing the language choices the author has made in writing that passage. By analyzing the lexical and grammatical features of a textbook passage, ELLs focus on the choices historians make in writing about history, on the way different meanings are presented, and on how important historical meanings are constructed. The grammatical characteristics of the discourse of history that make the text abstract and difficult to follow, such as nominalizations, choice of verbs and ways of reasoning, ambiguity of conjunctions and time reference, and lack of explicit explanations, become a focus of discussion as students analyze texts to unpack these meanings and understand the ambiguities.
>
> (Schleppegrell et al., 2004, pp. 76–7)

Schleppegrell and de Oliveira (2006) provide information about the ways teachers were introduced to this approach:

> In order to help teachers talk with students about how the language constructs a complex and dense passage like this one, we introduced them to some linguistic constructs that enable a focus on the meanings that the historian has embedded in this text. Teachers learned to divide sentences into their constituents and identify the meaning relationships among the constituents, to unpack the sometimes hidden meanings in complex nominal groups, to recognize how connectors and time phrases help structure a text, and to identify the chains of reference devices that are used to make cohesive links. By engaging in this as a group during the summer institutes, and then applying the same tools to analysis of passages relevant to their own classroom contexts, teachers learned how to guide their students to see the relevance of the language choices of the historian.
>
> (Schleppegrell & de Oliveira, 2006, p. 259) ■

The teachers in the California History Project were working in mainstream classrooms where L2 learners of varying proficiency levels were present in significant numbers. One common practice of these teachers was the use of metalanguage to engage students in identification of sentence constituents, with visual supports to help students see how a text is constructed and explore its meanings. For example, Table 4.1, adapted from Schleppegrell and de Oliveira (2006, p. 260), provides a deconstructed display of a paragraph about the Industrial Revolution:

> The Industrial Revolution shifted the world balance of power. It promoted competition between industrialized nations and increased poverty in less developed nations.
>
> **Rise of global inequality** Industrialization widened the gap between industrialized and non-industrialized countries, even while it strengthened their economic ties. To keep factories running and workers fed, industrialized countries required a steady supply of raw materials from less developed lands. In turn, industrialized countries viewed poor countries as markets for their manufactured products. A large inequality developed between the industrialized West and the rest of the world.
>
> (Beck, Black, Krieger, Naylor, & Shabaka, 2003, p. 266)

Table 4.1 provides a deconstructed perspective on the history passage by dividing each clause into its participants, processes, circumstances, and connectors. A look at the first Participant column highlights the role of the Industrial Revolution, industrialization, and industrialized countries in the actions presented in the processes. The second Participant column helps students recognize the effects of those actions. The circumstances focus on differences between industrialized nations and less developed nations throughout the text. Talking about how the participants, processes, and circumstances interact keeps the focus on meaning relevant to understanding the passage. Deconstructing the text in this way also helps students see how the grammar works. For example, their attention can be drawn to how 'to keep running' is a meaningful segment with 'factories' as the object, even though 'factories' interrupts the verb group 'to keep factories running'. In this infinitive clause, as in the text about Rome we looked at in Activity 4.1, the entity that keeps them running, 'industrialized countries', doesn't appear until later in the sentence, following the two actions, 'keep factories running' and 'workers fed'.

Connector	Participant	Process	Participant	Circumstance
	The Industrial Revolution	shifted	the world balance of power.	
	It (the Industrial Revolution)	promoted	competition	between industrialized nations
and	(the Industrial Revolution)	increased	poverty	in less developed nations.
	Industrialization	widened	the gap	between industrialized and non-industrialized countries,
even while	it (industrialization)	strengthened	their (industrialized and non-industrialized countries') economic ties.	
	(industrialized countries)	To keep … running	factories	
and	(industrialized countries)	(to keep) … fed,	workers	
	industrialized countries	required	a steady supply of raw material	from less developed lands.
In turn,	industrialized countries	viewed	poor countries	as markets for their (industrialized countries') manufactured products.
	A large inequality	developed		between the industrialized West and the rest of the world.

Table 4.1 Example of grammatical analysis (adapted from Schleppegrell & de Oliveira, 2006)

Developing the chart helps students recognize where participants and processes such as 'industrialized countries' and 'to keep' are assumed but not explicitly presented in the grammar; they can be 'recovered' and listed in parentheses, as in Table 4.1, making the meaning clearer. A focus on the connectors helps students understand the meaning of 'even while' and 'in turn' and the relationships they construct between clauses and sentences. Adding the pronoun referents—for example, 'It' ('the Industrial

Revolution') in the second row—gives students practice in linking from the pronoun back to the corresponding noun.

Teachers and students can use the deconstructed texts and charts to talk about these features and the ways they present historical knowledge, providing opportunities for students to engage more deeply with the text and begin to recognize patterns in the grammar that they will encounter in other history texts. This work also provides the basis for a discussion that can support the development of critical language awareness, as shown in Classroom Snapshot 4.1.

Classroom Snapshot 4.1

Teachers in the California History Project asked their tenth grade students to 'unravel' a text about the Vietnam War. Here's the text:

> The Viet Cong lacked the sophisticated equipment of the United States troops, so they avoided head-on clashes. Instead they used guerrilla warfare tactics, working in small groups to launch sneak attacks and practice sabotage. They often frustrated American search parties by hiding themselves in elaborate underground tunnels. Some of these were equipped with running water and electricity. The largest contained hospitals, stores, and weapons storage facilities.
>
> (…)
>
> In April 1966 the Americans introduced the huge B-52 bomber into the war to smash roads and heavy bridges in North Vietnam. During air raids these planes could drop thousands of tons of explosives over large areas. This saturation bombing tore North Vietnam apart.
>
> Many of the bombs used in these raids threw pieces of their thick metal casings in all directions when they exploded. These fragmentation bombs were not confined to the north alone. They were also used in the south, where they killed and maimed countless civilians.
>
> (Cayton et al., 2002, p. 623)

Students were asked to fill in a chart like Table 4.2, identifying whom or what the historian presents as the actor and receiver of action.

Reflecting on the analysis displayed in the chart, students were asked to answer these questions:

1 In the FIRST excerpt, in general, who or what are the PARTICIPANTS, the actors?
2 In the SECOND and THIRD excerpts, in general, who or what are the PARTICIPANTS, the actors?

Actor	Action process	Receiver of action or circumstances
The Viet Cong	avoided	head-on clashes
they (the Viet Cong)	used	guerrilla warfare tactics
they (the Viet Cong)	working … to launch	sneak attacks
they (the Viet Cong)	practice	sabotage
they (the Viet Cong)	often frustrated	American search parties
the Americans	introduced	the huge B-52 bomber
(the huge B-52 bomber)	to smash	roads and heavy bridges
these planes	could drop	thousands of tons of explosives
This saturation bombing	tore apart	North Vietnam
Many of the bombs used in these raids	threw	pieces of their thick metal casings in all directions
they	exploded	
?????	also used	these fragmentation bombs
they (these fragmentation bombs)	killed and maimed	countless civilians

Table 4.2 The representation of historical actors in a textbook

The questions the teachers are interested in are: 'What is the historian's perspective on these events? Who is acting? Who is presented as having agency?' The teachers are focused on helping students recognize a bias in this text. As we see, the agentive actors in the first part of the text are the Viet Cong, who are represented as using guerrilla tactics to attack Americans. What the class notices through this activity is that in the second and third parts of the text, it is mainly the bombs, not the Americans, who are given agency as actors. In fact, the actors who used the fragmentation bombs are not identified, as passive voice is used to present this without an explicit actor ('Many of the bombs used in these raids … '). ▪

Achugar, Schleppegrell, and Oteíza (2007) report that the teachers found this focus on language very powerful, as 'the students recognized that the author showed a bias in the way historical actors were presented' (p. 15). In addition, the teachers asked the students to think about how the language could have been used differently to present an alternative perspective. The teachers reported that this work supported their students in paying closer attention to language and noted that the students would not have had this discussion about historical agency without the support of the language analysis activity.

De Oliveira (2010) shows how analysis of grammar can help students recognize how cohesion is created as knowledge is built up in history texts through the use of complex nominalizations. As indicated above, a common pattern in the grammar of history texts is the use of nominalizations and complex noun groups in explanations about historical events. The texts of secondary schooling pack lots of information into each sentence as they present the knowledge students are expected to learn. Unpacking the complex noun groups and nominalizations can help students both better understand the content and learn about patterns of grammar through which explanations are constructed and meanings are built up.

In the following text about events leading to World War II, the italicized nominalizations and complex noun groups are used to summarize and reiterate central ideas:

Hitler Defies Versailles Treaty

Hitler had long pledged to undo the Versailles Treaty. Among its provisions, the treaty limited the size of Germany's army. In March 1935, the Führer announced that Germany would not obey these restrictions. In fact, Germany had already begun rebuilding its armed forces. The League issued only a mild condemnation. (…)

The League's failure to stop Germany from rearming convinced Hitler to take even greater risks. The treaty had forbidden German troops to enter a 30-mile-wide zone on either side of the Rhine River. Known as the Rhineland, it formed a buffer zone between Germany and France. It was also an important industrial area. On March 7, 1936, German troops moved into the Rhineland. Stunned, the French were willing to risk war. The British urged appeasement, giving in to an aggressor to keep peace.

Hitler later admitted that he would have backed down if the French and British had challenged him. *The German reoccupation of the Rhineland* marked a turning point in the march toward war. First, it strengthened Hitler's power and prestige within Germany. Cautious generals who had urged restraint now agreed to follow him. Second, the balance of power changed in Germany's favor. France and Belgium were now open to attack from German troops. Finally, *the weak response by France and Britain* encouraged Hitler to speed up his military and territorial expansion.

Hitler's growing strength convinced Mussolini that he should seek an alliance with Germany. In October 1936, the two dictators reached an agreement that became known as the Rome-Berlin Axis. A month later,

Germany also made an agreement with Japan. Germany, Italy, and Japan came to be called the Axis Powers.

(Beck et al., 2003, pp. 432–4)

The first paragraph's last sentences, '(...) Germany had already begun rebuilding its armed forces. The League issued only a mild condemnation', present information that is referred to in the first sentence of the second paragraph as 'The League's failure to stop Germany from rearming'. By condensing the meaning in this way, the writer can move forward with a sentence that tells what happened as a result. This is a frequent pattern in history that enables explanations to advance, as a point that has been made is restated in a nominalization or complex noun group. Students can explore such grammatical patterns by linking nominalizations and complex noun groups back to the information that is included and reiterated in them. The use of bold and italics in these sentences show this connection, linking the rebuilding of Germany's armed forces and the issuing of a mild condemnation to 'the League's failure to stop Germany from rearming':

> In fact, **Germany** had already begun **rebuilding its armed forces.** *The League issued only a mild condemnation.*

> *The League's failure* to stop **Germany** from **rearming** convinced Hitler to take even greater risks.

The nominalization is used as the actor of the sentence; this account suggests that it was '[t]he League's failure to stop Germany from rearming' that 'convinced' Hitler to 'take even greater risks'. By presenting the nominalization as doing the action of convincing, the author uses abstraction to repackage information from previous clauses while at the same time enabling the expansion and development of the explanation.

Activity 4.2

Three other complex noun groups are italicized in the text *Hitler Defies Versailles Treaty*. Where are the ideas in those complex noun groups introduced into the text? Identify the information that has been condensed from whole clauses into nominalizations. How do these summarize and reiterate central ideas in this text?

To understand the meaning of 'The German reoccupation of the Rhineland', the reader needs to look back to the second paragraph and understand that 'German troops moved into the Rhineland' is another way to say the same thing. As this was a key moment in the movement toward war, it is critical for understanding the text.

To comprehend the meaning of 'the weak response by France and Britain', the reader needs to understand the following sentences as constituting 'the weak response': 'Stunned, the French were willing to risk war. The British urged appeasement, giving in to an aggressor to keep peace.' The chain of reference here is not clearly signaled, so unpacking these nominalizations and relating them back to the information they condense and refer to is a complex but valuable endeavor.

Finally, 'Hitler's growing strength' is a complex noun group that refers back to the last words of the previous paragraph: that Hitler sped up 'his military and territorial expansion', along with other information in the previous paragraph, such as that his own generals now supported him and the German army now had the advantage.

The four nominalizations and complex noun groups we have been analyzing are key for understanding the evolving meaning in this passage:

- 'the League's failure to stop Germany from rearming'
- 'The German reoccupation of the Rhineland'
- 'the weak response by France and Britain'
- 'Hitler's growing strength'

Nominalizations and complex noun groups are the grammatical means through which abstraction and evaluation are built into this text. Students' ability to read and understand such constructions, as well as use them themselves, is crucial to their success in learning history and other secondary school subjects.

The role of a metalanguage is to provide a means of abstracting from the actual wording to the larger categories of meaning that form the grammatical systems of the language. In the examples in the text above and those included in Table 4.1, the metalanguage of *process, participant, circumstance, connector, reference,* and *nominalization* has been used to enable talk about historical agency, logical connections, and cohesive links across texts. Using this meaning-based metalanguage helps learners begin to recognize patterns in grammar and relate different patterns of form to the meanings they present.

As we saw in Chapter 3, teachers using functional grammar have found it beneficial at times to bridge the more traditional metalanguage (for example, *subjects* and *verbs*) and the more functional metalanguage (for example, *participants* and *processes*) (de Oliveira & Dodds, 2010). In Classroom Snapshot 4.2, we will see how a teacher has used more traditional metalanguage within a functional grammar approach.

Classroom Snapshot 4.2

In an English Language Development class, a kind of sheltered instruction for tenth to twelfth grade students in California, the teacher used Table 4.3 to help students explore a text. In this case, they were looking at how the author of a text about the famous labor organizer Cesar Chavez constructed evaluation of him and his movement:

Sentence analysis			
Before the subject	Subject	Verb	After the verb
During the 20th century	Cesar Chavez	was	a leading voice for migrant farm workers.
	His tireless leadership	focused	national attention on these laborers' terrible working conditions.
	This work	(eventually) led to	improvements.
However,	migrant farm workers	(still) face	many challenges in their daily lives.

Table 4.3 Sentence analysis (from Spycher, 2007, p. 248)

In the words of the teacher (who is also the researcher):

> Using the sentence analysis graphic organizer, I asked the students to consider questions such as whether the text had sentences containing more than one clause, what came first in clauses or sentences, how clauses were linked (e.g., with conjunctions, references, or adverbs), and how noun phrases were elaborated. I modeled, explained, and guided the students in the analyses. The students reported that this exercise helped them to better understand the texts they were reading, because it made certain linguistic features stand out.
>
> (Spycher, 2007, p. 248)

Spycher used traditional metalanguage to engage students in talk about the grammatical choices the text's author has made. However, she still showed that the purposes these grammatical features serve were meaningful in enabling an author to be authoritative and present Chavez and the migrant farm workers in particular ways. Bridging into some concepts from functional grammar, Spycher also asked students to look at the verbs in the independent clauses and classify them according to their meaning in context: whether they were presenting processes of *action* (*doing*), *thinking/feeling*, *saying*, or *being/having*. When verb phrases included modal verbs, the class discussed the meaning contributed by the modal and the purpose for which the author used it. As we discussed in Chapter 2, modality is an important resource for interpersonal meaning. Spycher points out that this kind of exercise was useful for showing students how writers establish an authoritative stance by using the resources of modality (for example, 'it is necessary to' and 'must') to guide their readers to see things in a certain way.

According to Spycher, this activity helped students think about verb choices in new ways as they began to recognize that different words serve different functions in conveying meaning. She reports the point made by one student, who said:

> *Para una persona que aprende un lenguaje diferente al suyo, es importante saber las funciones de las palabras* [For a person who is learning a different language, it's important to know the functions of words]

(Spycher, 2007, p. 249) ■

Activity 4.3

Look at the verbs in the example from Spycher in Table 4.3. How would you classify the four verbs used in the text about Cesar Chavez and what are their functions?

In the first sentence, 'was' presents a being process that functions to introduce and identify Cesar Chavez. 'Focused' presents an action process, and it is interesting to note that the 'actor' in this process is 'his tireless leadership'. This offers the opportunity to draw students' attention to the fact that abstract notions like 'leadership' are nominalized forms (turning 'leads' into 'leadership'), common in academic texts. Use of this nominalized form enables the writer to evaluate Chavez by adding the adjective 'tireless'. 'Focused' is an abstract action, used here to construct a relationship between Chavez's 'tireless leadership' and 'these laborers' working conditions'. In the following sentence, 'led to', a verb form often used in writing about history, enables the writer to bring 'time' and 'cause' together to show the results of Chavez's leadership. In that sentence, the demonstrative 'This work' refers back to 'tireless leadership'. The final sentence also uses a being process, 'face', to present the ongoing reality of the challenges that remain for farm workers. Analyzing and talking about authorial choices such as these can help students recognize ways of writing more authoritatively. In particular, it can help them draw on the grammatical resources of being and doing processes to present abstraction and evaluation.

As explained in Chapters 2 and 3, the notion of a mode continuum is useful for thinking about the multiple ways teachers can support students' grammatical development through different types of tasks. Gibbons (2008) offers many examples from her research with L2 learners in middle school history and science to illustrate how students can be engaged in exploring differences in spoken and written grammar by transferring information into different registers/modes. The ability to use nominalization is crucial for this. For example, Gibbons describes how a teacher engages her seventh grade science students in repackaging their knowledge in more authoritative language. As they talk about the value of repeating a science experiment, she recasts 'do it many times' and 'kept doing it' into the more authoritative 'replication' in order to help them talk in more technical ways.

Spycher (2007) describes how instruction in deconstructing text can progress from explicit teacher modeling and explanation to practice. This practice can include opportunities for peer collaborative work. Later, once students are ready to use their new understanding to write about what they have learned, it can take the form of independent practice. In treating writing as a process of multiple drafts and revisions, Spycher helped students jointly revise their own and each other's texts by considering the grammatical differences between everyday and more academic ways of presenting information in their writing and moving back and forth in their talk along the mode continuum. Below is an example of the kind of revision she supported:

Student writing:

Rosa Parks was famous because she fought for the black people to stop racism in Montgomery, Alabama.

Revision (jointly constructed with teacher guiding the class):

Rosa Parks' fight against racism was an important part of the civil rights movement.

(Spycher, 2007, p. 249)

Here, the teacher helps to revise a student's multi-clause construction by using a nominalization to turn it into a one-clause sentence. This enables the student to say not only that Parks' fame came from her work against racism but also that her fight against racism contributed in important ways to the civil rights movement. The teacher here helps construct a nominalization ('Rosa Parks' fight against racism') that allows the information presented in the student's draft to be evaluated in the same clause. This is the same use of nominalization that we saw in the Cesar Chavez example: 'his tireless leadership'. As Spycher notes, this kind of work shows students how to do two things: firstly, how to foreground the struggle against racism, rather than Rosa Parks as a person, by placing it as the subject of the sentence; and secondly, how to authoritatively set up her fight as something to be evaluated. Furthermore, instead of evaluating Rosa Parks as famous, the nominalization enables the writer to evaluate the struggle against racism as important.

Revision of this kind involves more than just fixing grammatical errors in students' writing. Instead, it involves introducing students to new patterns of grammar that they can use to write more effectively. Teachers who understand how and why valued academic writing often uses nominalizations can introduce students to patterns of grammar that enable them to be more authoritative in their writing (Macken-Horarik, 1996).

As we saw in this section, grammar can and should be addressed through reading. Teachers can be proactive about what to include in their grammar instruction by selecting grammar points in texts L2 learners read and thus drawing their attention to how grammar is used in particular contexts. This supports development of grammatical knowledge, text comprehension, and critical literacy. We have also introduced the notion that student writing can be supported by this kind of grammar teaching. The next section of this chapter expands on this, providing further insight into ways of supporting L2 learners' grammatical development in writing. This movement in classroom activities from deconstruction of text, through talk about grammar in what students read, to their use of the grammatical resources in their own writing is, of course, the goal of the focus on grammar. Learners need to take knowledge they develop through reading and be able to represent it in written texts. Writing also gives learners individual opportunities for output in the context of meaningful work in the subject area.

Learning Grammar for Writing Secondary School Subjects

In this section, we review research that helps us understand how teachers can focus on grammar while preparing students to write the challenging texts of secondary schooling. As we do so, we will consider how talk about grammar can support preparation for writing and help move students into control of academic registers.

Spotlight Study 4.2

A major research effort is currently underway in Europe, where an approach to language learning called Content and Language Integrated Learning (CLIL) is increasing in popularity. Its goal is to ensure that EU citizens have competence in two other European Community languages besides their mother tongue (European Commission, 1995). In CLIL programs, the language of instruction is a foreign language which is not present in students' local communities. Llinares et al. (2012) report on analysis of classroom interaction in CLIL programs in Spain,

Austria, Finland, and the Netherlands, where English, a foreign language, is used as a medium of instruction. A main focus is on helping students write the valued genres of secondary schooling. The researchers describe ways teachers are engaging students in talk in preparation for writing, with the talk serving as a kind of oral rehearsal for presenting the information they are learning. Classroom Snapshot 4.3 is an example of interaction between a teacher and student in this context:

Classroom Snapshot 4.3

In this excerpt from a Grade 8 history classroom, the (13–14-year-old) students are discussing what life was like in feudal Europe:

Student: Serfs … without pay, remuneration, they don't pay them and the free peasants they … they give them money.

Teacher: OK. And … em … about serfs, XX they were similar to something. I hope you remember.

Student: The slaves.

Teacher: To slaves.

Student: Were property of someone.

(Llinares et al., 2012, p. 193)

We see here that the student is struggling to talk about the status of serfs. But in reporting a series of contrasting actions to compare serfs and free peasants ('they don't pay them'; 'they give them money'), the student cannot reach the generalization about serfs that he is trying to make. By refocusing the grammatical form and introducing a different sentence structure ('they were similar to something'), the teacher engages in a move that pushes the student toward more abstract generalization about the position of serfs. Instead of 'they don't pay them', the student recasts the information as 'they were property of someone'. This substitutes a being process ('were similar to') for the doing processes ('pay' and 'give') the student used first. (Following Halliday (1994), Llinares et al. refer to being processes as 'relational processes', and doing processes as 'material processes'.) Whittaker and Llinares (2009) found that CLIL students used more being processes in their writing about a topic than in their spoken discussion on the same topic in class, and attribute this in part to the teacher's role in scaffolding the use of being processes in the classroom talk. ■

As we saw in the review of Spycher's work, being processes are often key to presenting information in authoritative and academic ways. A move toward command of being processes that pack information into noun groups becomes important in secondary schooling in order that students learn to engage with more abstract and theoretical knowledge. Movement back and forth along the mode continuum supports development of the ability to take a doing process and evaluate it by recasting it as a nominalization. (For example, 'They didn't get any money' can be restated and developed as 'Their lack of resources led them to rebel'.)

Activity 4.4

Look again at Classroom Snapshot 4.3 (see page 102) in light of Gibbons' mode-shifting moves (1 'talking about language, using meaningful metalanguage'; 2 'unpacking written language'; 3 'recasting student discourse'; 4 'reminding and handing over'). Which of the moves can be observed in this interaction?

There are two acts of teacher recasting in this episode. First, the student's contribution is recast into a whole new sentence structure: 'they were similar to something'. This recasting offers the students new grammatical resources for making a generalization. Such recasting into more academically valued forms is an important way teachers can support L2 learners in moving from everyday registers into academic ones. In addition, the teacher recasts the student's response to the prompting from 'The slaves' to 'To slaves' to reinforce the structure 'similar to'—a more familiar kind of recasting that restates what the student has said in more accurate grammatical form.

The episode is also an example of 'reminding and handing over'. The student is obviously already familiar with the structure 'is similar to'; the teacher's scaffolding serves as a reminder that the structure is going to be useful here. In fact, the student is able to take this cue and formulate the idea in a more generalized way.

We can see the challenge of academic language in a second or foreign language when we compare the grammatical resources students have for construing knowledge in their L1s to what they can often draw on in their L2s. The CLIL research reported above also offers an example from Llinares and Whittaker (2010) of responses to the same question about the Black Death by students studying the topic in their (Spanish) L1 and in the CLIL classroom. The question is why the plague spread so rapidly. The student using L1 replies '*Por el hacinamiento* [Due to overcrowding]', while the CLIL student responds 'Because the people are not clean' (Llinares et al., 2012, p. 196). This is not just a vocabulary difference. The student in the L1 context uses a structure more common in written academic language to present causal information: the prepositional phrase 'due to' and an abstract noun. In contrast, the CLIL student uses a whole clause with the conjunction 'because' and more everyday language. The student speaking in L1 is using the resources of academic language in Spanish by drawing on nominalization ('*el hacinamiento*') to express the idea as an abstraction. These register choices are not yet developed in the student using L2. The authors suggest that a key role of secondary school teachers should be to help students develop the ability to use nominalizations to produce sentence structures that make their language more academic in both written and spoken modes.

Moving Students into Grammar for Academic Registers

In addition to nominalization, there are other grammatical forms that secondary-level learners need to control for success in academic registers (spoken and written). This section highlights some of the other grammatical forms required for more advanced written tasks in the secondary years, including conjunction, reference, and causal language. Teaching these forms involves moving back and forth on the mode continuum, helping students use first oral language and then written language to present disciplinary meanings more authoritatively.

For example, Gibbons (2008) describes how, through joint construction with students, the teacher helped seventh grade L2 learners of English move between everyday ways of talking and more abstract ways of writing about their experience:

> [T]he students were asked to think about how they would complete sentences such as 'When I left my country I left …'; 'When I came to Australia I found …'; 'When I came to this school I found …'; 'As I leave this school I feel …'. Through a joint construction with the students, the teacher recoded the students' everyday language ('friends', 'sad', 'happy', 'free') into more abstract terms such as 'friendship', 'sadness', 'joy', 'freedom', and 'harmony'. These terms were used in a music concert that marked the end of most of the participating students' time at the school, in which many of the students performed. Transformation here worked at many levels: from personal experiences expressed in 'everyday' language to generalisable abstractions expressed as nominalisations; from the expression of ideas in students' first languages to their second language; and from shared classroom learning to the context of a performance with an audience.
>
> (Gibbons, 2008, p. 163)

Such instruction shows how vocabulary and grammar interact, as the whole sentence structure often requires shifts in making this move toward abstraction.

Another grammatical challenge for students at this level is using conjunctions in effective and meaningful ways. Conjunctions, as we saw in Chapter 3, are an important resource for structuring discourse, and even in the early grades, it is important for teachers to help students learn to use conjunctions that are common in academic language but not so common in everyday talk. In the secondary years, students are expected to control a wider range of conjunctions and conjunctive meanings, and teachers can be alert to opportunities to support students' development of appropriate conjunctive resources.

The CLIL studies discussed above provide an example of a teacher who misses an opportunity to highlight the correct use of conjunction. In talking about the role of a dowry in feudal Europe, the student says: '… they dowry her to a nobleman and they pay him … eh … for marry with her.' The teacher responds: 'Yes. They give a dowry.' (Llinares et al., 2012, p. 194). Here, the teacher focuses on the use of 'dowry' and recasts it as a noun and not a verb, but the incorrect expression of the logical meaning is not addressed, as the purpose relationship in the sentence needs to be expressed as 'in order to', not 'for'. While, of course, teachers cannot recast every such infelicitous example, being alert to how logical relationships are expressed can become a focus both in response to students' talk and writing and in deconstructing and exploring grammar in the texts students read.

Similarly, students tend to draw on everyday conjunctions when more academic ones are needed. Llinares et al. (2012) provide an example of a student whose spoken report uses 'and' multiple times rather than the contrastive and consequential conjunctions that would better express the meanings between the clauses:

> they had the agriculture (…) and they develop a new economy, and the salary grows for the people because in … they were eh … less people, the salary grows for the people who work.
>
> (Llinares et al., 2012, p. 195)

The first 'and' links two clauses that might more felicitously be linked with 'but', 'then', or another contrastive meaning. The second 'and' could be more effectively replaced with a conjunction of consequence ('*so* the salary grows'). Llinares and Whittaker (2010) report that the CLIL students more frequently drew on 'and' than students working at the same level and on the same topics in their L1 (Spanish). To respond to this frequent use of coordination, mainly through 'and', they suggest that teachers raise students' awareness of the different meanings that 'and' is expected to carry here and in other such student writing. This would not only improve their production in the L2 but would also help them comprehend texts they encounter where more academic conjunctions are used.

Work with conjunctions has also been reported in research on **sentence combining**, an approach where students are encouraged to put ideas together in more complex sentences. Shin (2009) reports on an investigation of sentence combining with high school L2 students as part of a larger project on academic language development. Students practiced rewriting sentences and discussed their justifications for their grammatical and rhetorical choices, with multiple solutions encouraged. Shin reports that this work:

> provided occasions for "student-initiated preemptive focus-on-form" (Ellis et al., 2002) and immediate instructor feedback, which clarified meaning and use of certain structures and directly addressed gaps in the students' grammar knowledge (Ellis, 2002). It helped the stronger students to solidify their knowledge of certain grammatical structures by justifying their choices and negotiating meanings.
>
> (Shin, 2009, p. 401)

Shin's study illustrates the critical role a teacher plays in drawing students' attention to form even as they engage in meaningful discussion.

Spycher (2007), discussed above in reference to nominalization and complex noun groups, also includes work on conjunction as a crucial support for L2 learners. The title of her article, 'Academic writing of adolescent English learners: Learning to use "although"', comes from a question asked by Ernesto, a tenth grade student from Mexico who had been in the USA for only a short time:

> *Maestra, ¿qué quiere decir 'although' en español?* [Teacher, what does 'although' mean in Spanish?]
>
> (Spycher, 2007, p. 239)

Spycher points out that this question is not simple to answer: what is important to understand in using conjunctions is how they function to make particular kinds of logical connections in text, so that just giving a gloss related to the meaning is insufficient to help learners use them effectively. With 'although', the writer is typically bringing in information already presented in the text or context in order to acknowledge or concede a point but then go beyond it in the next clause to make a further point. Learning both the meaning of conjunctions and how to use them appropriately is challenging, and Spycher provides an example of the ways Ernesto learns to revise his text for greater effectiveness.

Activity 4.5

Here are excerpts from the two versions of an essay on the 2006 tsunami written by Ernesto, Spycher's focal student. What changes do you see in these sentences? How might the ways of teaching grammar described in this book have supported the revision?

First draft:

The people of the others countries are helping. Although the help can't give all the people. It is almost impossible to help everyone.

(Spycher, 2007, p. 247)

Revision:

The world is helping now with food, money, clean water, and clothing. Although this help is necessary, it is impossible to help everybody.

(Spycher, 2007, p. 250)

We see in Ernesto's revision that he has expanded the first sentence to include more information about how the world is helping victims of the tsunami. In his second sentence, he uses the noun group 'this help' instead of 'the help', making the reference more cohesive. By distilling 'food', 'money', 'clean water', and 'clothing' into the two words 'this help', he is able to refer back as well as to move forward and develop his point. (See Spycher, 2007, for examples of how the teacher supported students' understanding of the grammar of reference.) In his first draft, it is not clear how he understands the meaning contributed by 'although', using it in a similar way to 'but'. In his revision, Ernesto is able to use 'although' more effectively to make the point that even with this aid, some people will still need help. Spycher acknowledges that Ernesto still has much to learn, but argues that the deconstruction of text and talk about grammar has helped him begin to adopt the academic register features he will need to be a successful writer in his content classes.

Whittaker (2010) provides examples of how a student's grammatical resources develop over time with support for talk about grammar in the context of reading and writing in a CLIL classroom. Her particular focus is on the grammar of causal language. Below are examples of writing by the same student over three years:

Year One

The civilizations were so important because the most powerful people stood there and because they were the main sources of work and culture.

(Whittaker, 2010, p. 34)

This is an 'everyday' way of presenting causes, introducing the causes with the conjunction 'because'. This is typically the first way students begin to control this grammatical meaning.

Year Three: Example 1

At that time poor people didn't have resources to develop and rich people became richer with the rise of taxes and prices during the Inflation after mercantilism.

(Whittaker, 2010, p. 35)

Here, the student presents cause in the prepositional phrase 'with the rise of taxes and prices during the Inflation after mercantilism'. Using the prepositional phrase enables the writer to adopt a more academic voice than would be possible using 'because'. A sentence with 'because' (for example, 'rich people became richer because taxes and prices rose during the Inflation after mercantilism') would not be wrong, but it would have a clause-chaining style that presents less information in each clause. Using 'with' enables the writer to construct a complex noun group rather than a clause, presenting the more authoritative stance valued in academic written language.

Year Three: Example 2

Another important cause was the differences of costums, languages and traditions in the balcans that led to many crisis.

(Whittaker, 2010, p. 35)

In this example, the student uses the nominal form 'another important cause', making the notion of cause the point of departure for the sentence, and draws on the verb 'led to', a resource, as we saw above, that enables the conflation of time and cause in history discourse. These lexical and grammatical developments indicate that the writer is gaining control of the grammar of history discourse.

Writing instruction is a powerful context for addressing grammar, as teachers can be proactive in identifying grammatical points to discuss with L2 learners when they write, and can tailor their feedback to the particular issues each student is grappling with. To do this well, teachers need to understand the kinds of language choices that are relevant to accomplishing the writing tasks they are asking their students to perform.

Summary

The research reviewed here has shown how grammar can be taught in the contexts of meaningful work on secondary school subjects. This research provides a basis for understanding how subject-area texts draw on grammar in particular ways, and for recognizing how this grammar becomes more dense, technical, and abstract as students move from the primary to secondary years.

In this chapter we have offered additional examples of students engaged in text deconstruction to identify meaningful grammatical segments and their functions. We have focused on some key grammatical features of the texts students encounter in secondary school:

- *infinitive clauses* and *participial clauses* that do not have agentive participants, to help learners recognize when they need to look ahead in the text for information
- *nominalizations* and *complex noun groups* that distill and re-present information that has been developed in a text
- the ways *cohesive reference* is developed across a text through pronouns, nominalizations, and other reference devices so that the presentation and development of information can be tracked
- analysis of *participants* and *passive voice* that enables students to recognize agency
- *conjunctions* that present academic meanings and develop the logic of a text
- *being processes* and *nominal forms* that enable evaluative meaning to be built into a clause and allow meanings such as cause to be made without conjunctions.

These are grammatical resources that facilitate the construction of authoritative explanations and arguments in the texts of secondary school. We have seen that helping students notice these patterns in language supports their critical reading and gives them tools they can use in their own writing.

Learners' awareness of these language features and their forms and meanings can be supported with use of metalanguage that enables discussion about the grammatical choices authors make and the meanings those choices present. We have illustrated how these features can be in focus through the use of both traditional and functional metalanguage.

Teachers can be proactive in focusing students on grammatical patterns in both comprehension and language production. Students' explicit attention can be drawn to the grammatical patterns in the reading that they do and the writing they are asked to perform. We have seen examples of the ways teachers can move students across the mode continuum through talk about text, talk to support oral rehearsal before writing, and then writing tasks that enable students to use the new grammatical forms. We have seen how both in deconstructing written text and in compacting spoken language, students can explore and play with the grammar along the mode continuum, packaging meaning in the looser structures of spoken language and then repackaging the meanings in ways more valued in written academic language.

A functional grammar approach is of greatest value in addressing the needs of students in the secondary school, as it is at this age that they need the register flexibility to adapt their language to a variety of purposes across subject areas. Accurate L2 production does not suffice if the language choices being made do not engage with the abstraction, evaluation, and theorizing expected in the more advanced texts students are required to produce at this level. We have seen how teachers can make the discursive patterns and practices of their subject areas explicit to L2 learners, and guide them to formulate meaning in new ways to achieve content expectations. Teachers who are able to do this offer learners powerful support in developing the kind of L2 proficiency they need for success in school and beyond.

5 Grammar Teaching: What We Know Now

Preview

In this chapter, we return to the statements about grammar teaching that you responded to in Activity 1.1. For each statement, we provide a response based on the research that has been presented in this book. Before you read our responses, review your own ideas by returning to your responses in Activity 1.1.

Activity 5.1: Review Your Opinions

In Activity 1.1 (page 8), you indicated how strongly you agreed with some statements about grammar teaching. Before you continue reading this chapter, go back and complete the questionnaire again. Compare the responses you gave then to those you would give now. Have your views about grammar teaching been changed or confirmed by what you've read in the preceding chapters?

Reflecting on Ideas about Grammar Teaching

1 Grammar is a set of rules about language use.

In Chapter 1, we showed how grammar can be thought of in different ways. When teaching grammar to L1 students, the focus is often on rules for correct use of language features in writing. Linguists often define grammar as the unconscious knowledge that native speakers have about language. These can both be helpful ways of thinking about grammar, but in this book we present a different perspective that we see as most relevant to L2 learning, defining grammar as a resource for making meaning in a new language.

This view of grammar teaching puts the functions of language at the forefront and enables teachers to make the development of L2 learners' grammatical resources their main focus. We have positioned teaching grammar as expanding L2 learners' linguistic repertoires so that they are able to use the new language to support their learning at school. By viewing grammar as a resource for meaning-making, teachers can draw L2 learners' attention to the kinds of choices speakers and writers make in accomplishing particular purposes in specific contexts. The focus is not on rules for correctness but on recognizing patterns in the ways language is used and on being able to see how the different grammatical systems are used to make meaning in different contexts.

2 Learning grammar means learning how to speak and write effectively in different contexts and situations.

In Chapter 1, we introduced an approach to planning for grammar instruction at the primary and secondary levels. The approach asks teachers to consider the language forms that will be prominent and functional for achieving the content purposes of the curriculum, and to direct talk about grammar toward helping students understand how those language forms are used and what they mean. This approach allows the grammar in focus to be a point of discussion across all of the learning activities in a unit of instruction so that its use can be modeled in speaking and writing. It also links the grammar with what it helps us accomplish in different subject areas and tasks.

We introduced the notion of Gibbons' mode continuum to highlight the different ways speakers and writers draw on the grammatical resources of a language when doing different things. This helps children recognize that the grammar we use depends on what it is we are doing with language, with whom we are interacting, what we are interacting about, and what our goals are in the interaction. For children learning an L2, the contexts in which they need support for learning are varied. This has been demonstrated by the range of activities in this book that have drawn attention to differences in subject areas, differences in the activities children engage in over a unit of study, and differences that depend on whom they are speaking with or the audience for which they are writing. Making these differences salient and a topic of discussion helps L2 learners recognize the grammatical choices they can make in different contexts to achieve different purposes.

By designing units of study that enable learners to engage with language in different ways, teachers can provide opportunities for learners to use informal language, explore the more formal language through which knowledge is presented to them in the texts they read, and draw on the new grammar to do the work of the content area. In making grammar a focus across these contexts, teachers support children in learning and using new grammatical forms. The grammatical focus shifts according to subject area, tasks, and learning context, helping learners see the variability in the choices available to them in the grammar.

Teaching grammar involves making L2 learners aware of the kinds of choices speakers and writers make in accomplishing their goals in particular contexts. This helps them learn about language variation and how different choices are appropriate for different purposes. L2 learners build their linguistic repertoires for meaning-making as they become more sensitive to the purposes and contexts that call for specific choices.

3 Grammar should be an ongoing focus of attention in L2 teaching.

The research presented in this book supports the view that explicit and ongoing attention to grammar, particularly for learners in communicative and content-based instructional settings, is essential to enable the levels of language development needed for success in school. We saw in the research reviewed in Chapter 2 that noticing and awareness-raising are of great importance in helping learners use a new language with authority and effectiveness. Planning for moving learners along the mode continuum offers teachers a way to think about how a sustained focus on grammar and language form–meaning connections can be implemented in the classroom. As students engage in different kinds of activities, the teacher can play an important role in mediating their learning by drawing their attention to the different ways language is used.

The mode continuum refers to movement between spoken and written language as well as movement between more everyday and more academic language. Gibbons suggests that movement back and forth across the mode continuum is important for supporting L2 students in making use of what they can already do with language and in learning to use new language resources. Throughout this book, we have asked you to think about four pedagogical moves that support talk and engagement with language across contexts of learning, drawing on Gibbons (2006a). These moves are:

1 'talking about language, using meaningful metalanguage'
2 'unpacking written language'
3 'recasting student discourse'
4 'reminding and handing over'.

The first pedagogical move—'talking about language, using meaningful metalanguage'—brings L2 learners' attention to the linguistic resources they need to achieve their purposes in a particular task. Your role as a teacher is to identify key grammatical features that could be addressed across a unit of instruction and plan ways of maintaining a focus on those features.

The second pedagogical move—'unpacking written language'—gives L2 learners opportunities to work with models of language as it is used in the texts they read and write, exploring the language choices an author makes and analyzing the systems of language through which meaning is presented. In 'unpacking written language', students are supported in moving along the mode continuum as they take written language and restate its meanings in ways that are more everyday or informal. Similarly, by repackaging the spoken language into the more formal and technical language of the content areas, students gain practice in using more academic ways of expressing their perspectives and presenting what they have learned. In developing understanding about how to make their language more formal or informal, they develop understanding about language variation and more flexibility in language use.

The third pedagogical move—'recasting student discourse'—brings a new meaning to the notion of recast, referring to moves teachers can make to respond to students' language production by restating their contributions in more authoritative, technical, or disciplinary discourse. This offers learners models of correct grammatical form as well as more appropriate, effective, or content-specific language forms.

The fourth pedagogical move—'reminding and handing over'—refers to planning for student production of language, where teachers ask learners to draw on the language that has been in focus in speech or writing and use it in new learning tasks that call for those language forms. The tasks teachers engage learners in when reminding and handing over can also serve as assessments of grammar learning, as they indicate whether the students have taken up the new grammatical forms and are using them effectively.

These four moves allow close attention to grammar while also supporting content learning for L2 learners. When grammar is seen as a resource for meaning-making, it can be an ongoing focus in L2 teaching, as the grammar teaching prompts reflection on language choices speakers and writers can make in accomplishing particular purposes in specific contexts. This can be an enjoyable and engaging activity for learners at all levels.

4 Grammar needs to be taught as a separate component of the curriculum.

What we have argued is that grammar has to be taught in the context of also teaching something else. We do not recommend teaching grammar in isolation from other teaching, but instead that it be infused into the curriculum across activities involving all language skills. When grammar is taught in isolation, students may not be able to apply what they have learned in authentic contexts of use. In this book, we have presented ways of teaching grammar in the L2 classroom that fully integrate it into instruction that addresses the larger classroom goals and curriculum. Subject-area instructional activities that teachers and students are already doing in classrooms offer important and authentic opportunities for explicit attention to the ways language works in its forms and meanings.

Given that stance, you may be surprised that we agree with the statement that grammar needs to be taught as a separate component! The approach presented here should not be interpreted to mean that no separate grammar instruction is needed. In fact, we have argued that grammar needs to have a central role in preparing teachers to work with children who are L2 learners, and teachers need to implement grammar instruction on an ongoing basis. Without a robust focus on grammar, learners will be denied opportunities to develop fully in the new language.

A language teacher does need to prepare for and support an explicit attention to grammar in the classroom. Since explicit attention to language itself is necessary for optimal L2 development, teachers need to be knowledgeable about grammar and form–meaning connections in the subject areas they teach. In order to situate grammar teaching in the context of teaching the texts students read, the writing they do, and the classroom activities in which they engage, teachers need to understand how language works in their subjects and which points of grammar are most important for students to reflect on and practice.

In Chapter 1, we offered frameworks for designing units of study in both the primary classroom and the secondary content classroom that integrate grammar teaching with content teaching. Since language is the means through which learning is constructed and evaluated in all subjects, addressing grammar in the content-area classroom makes the meaning-making resources visible and an ongoing focus of attention. As L2 learners engage in discussion about grammar, they also gain awareness about the way knowledge is constructed in language in different content areas.

5 Grammar can best be taught when teaching speaking and writing, that is, when learners are producing language.

To know whether learners have taken up the grammar that is taught, they need to engage in speaking and writing, producing the output that Swain's research, discussed in Chapter 2, shows is so important for learning. But as we have demonstrated in this book, grammar can also be taught in the context of developing students' receptive language skills, especially reading. Focusing learners on the ways grammar works in the texts they read across subject areas offers a rich context for teaching language systems that are relevant to the learning they are engaged in. For example, we saw how learners can identify the ways the systems of mood and speech function are used in authentic texts, and then discuss how commands and questions work and how they are structured. We explored examples in which teachers asked learners to look at how different verb phrases, or process types, present meanings of different kinds that enable particular functions. You read about how teachers can draw students' attention to the use of conjunctions and connectors in structuring texts, and how a focus on reference can help students track the introduction and development of concepts.

The texts children read can provide effective models and opportunities to identify and think about the ways language is used by authors in authentic contexts, as we have shown in Chapters 3 and 4. Opportunities for deconstructing text, talking about the forms and meanings used by the author, and then practicing making those same meanings develop L2 learners' understanding of the texts they read and support them in producing the texts they have to write. Through talk about the grammar of texts, teachers can develop L2 learners' awareness of how the grammatical systems work. We have shown how you can explore the grammar used in texts of different types through activities that engage L2 learners in moving from what they know to using new ways of expressing themselves.

6 Grammar instruction is provided in similar ways across grade levels.

This statement has two aspects to consider: the pedagogical approach to be used and the particular structures to target. From the perspective we have presented, we have argued that in both primary and secondary contexts, the teacher can initiate grammar instruction by identifying content goals and considering what students need to understand about grammar to achieve those goals. We have shown how teachers can look at the reading and writing students will be asked to do over a unit of study to identify grammatical features the learners will need to know and be able to use. Teachers can then plan a proactive focus on that grammar to identify, draw learners' attention to, and provide practice that builds up those language resources over the course of the unit. In that sense, the approach to grammar instruction can be similar across grade levels.

However, the grammatical features that teachers will need to attend to will vary across grade levels and subject areas. As we showed in Chapter 2, the grammar students encounter becomes more dense, abstract, and technical as they move through the school years. Therefore, being aware of how the demands of the grammar change over time is important for selecting grammar features that will help children be successful in their learning. Christie (2012) is a valuable resource for thinking about the ways the language that children need to draw on evolves over the years of schooling. For example, teachers can help primary school students explore verb meanings to recognize how a science report employs different kinds of verbs from a story, as described in Chapter 3. Chapter 4 illustrated how secondary school teachers can assist students in recognizing how grammatical agency is presented in history texts and in learning to use the more advanced conjunctive meanings necessary for authoritative writing. Other examples throughout this book have shown how different grammatical resources can be in focus to meet curriculum needs.

7 Knowing grammar rules is sufficient for being able to use grammar effectively.

Even when students know grammar rules, they are not always able to produce correct forms in contexts of use. And yet, as we saw in Chapter 2, language production is necessary to support language development. That means L2 learners need to make errors in order to grow in language proficiency; language production is itself a source of learning.

Language production actively promotes language development as it encourages noticing and enhances fluency through practice. Using language prompts L2 learners to draw on the forms they have learned, requiring them to focus on how they are expressing themselves. Through their language production, L2 learners test hypotheses about the new language and internalize new linguistic knowledge. Thus, successful grammar learning requires sustained attention to and production of the language to be learned through activities that push learners to focus on form and meaning. We have shown in this book how students can be pushed to speak and write in ways that enable them to make use of the grammar that is the target of instruction.

8 Grammar teaching means correcting students' errors.

Teaching grammar does, of course, involve correcting students' errors, but as we saw in Chapter 2, just providing corrective feedback is not sufficient for enabling learners to use the language accurately. Students need many opportunities to engage with the language to be learned and practice using it. But with a definition of grammar as a meaning-making resource, the emphasis in the classroom should be on meaning and development of new language resources rather than on correcting errors. The theory presented in Chapter 2 showed that what best supports language development is meaningful interaction, with frequent opportunities for learners to attend to and use new forms, guided by explicit talk about language and meaning. Drawing learners' attention to form–meaning connections and engaging them in meaningful use of the language are essential aspects of grammar instruction.

Both writing and speaking, through which learners can practice using new forms, offer potential contexts for correction. Traditional grammar teaching, with discrete-point presentation and practice of individual grammatical forms one at a time (for example, verb forms, plurals, verb tense, and other features), can be part of classroom instruction, with sentence-level practice using forms that have been in focus in meaningful contexts. When accuracy in language use is important, correction of grammatical form can best be done through activities such as writing tasks, where the learner can focus on the form and apply the rule.

But language learning is, at its core, the learning of new ways of making meaning in different contexts. Grammar teaching should therefore give priority to drawing learners' attention to patterns that they can incorporate into their linguistic knowledge, expanding their resources for meaning-making. We have suggested that grammar teaching in the K-12 classroom should focus on structures that will be used by L2 learners to make meaning in their content learning. This book has shown how you can provide opportunities for close attention to language as it is used in the instructional texts learners engage with, thus offering opportunities for students to see how forms are used in context and explore the relationship between form and meaning. We have proposed many ways of going beyond responding to errors as a means of teaching grammar.

9 Using grammatical terminology is an important part of teaching grammar.

L2 learners need explicit information about form–meaning connections, as this is an important aspect of raising awareness and promoting noticing. We have shown how grammatical metalanguage can support grammar instruction by providing an explicit focus on form and meaning, as particular instances of language use are related to the larger systems of which they are a part. Metalanguage can refer both to linguistic terminology and to talk about language.

Using grammatical metalanguage to engage L2 learners in talk about language and content supports curricular learning, as students recognize how language choices contribute to the meanings presented in a text. We have shown how the learning of technical metalanguage can be situated in meaningful contexts where it serves instructional content goals. Interaction about meaningful content using metalanguage assists L2 learners in analyzing patterns in the language that can be linked with categories of meaning. Drawing learners' attention to form–meaning connections plays an important role in moving them toward more advanced levels of language use.

Children are able to develop metalanguage from an early age, as we saw in Chapter 3. In this book, we have used some traditional linguistic terms, but we have also introduced functional metalanguage that more closely relates form and meaning. Learning to use new metalanguage, traditional or functional, is a skill that needs to be taught so that L2 learners are able to apply it in talking about language and meaning. Both types of metalanguage offer opportunities for learners to look at particular instances of language use and name the structures and meanings involved. Doing this helps them develop more generalized understanding about how language works and recognize systems and patterns of language when they encounter them in new contexts.

10 Teachers need to have deep knowledge about grammar in order to teach it.

We have shown that even without a lot of technical knowledge, you can explore grammar with your L2 learners in order to help them recognize how the new language works and learn new ways of using it. In fact, the teachers we have worked with have found that their own knowledge about grammar only deepens when they engage their students in the kinds of activities we have presented in this book. Learning grammar is a life-long enterprise, as every language has many complex grammatical systems that can be endlessly explored. So don't feel nervous about your own knowledge of grammar! Instead, select one of the systems we have illustrated here and begin to reflect on how it works in the texts you teach. Over time, you will become comfortable with that system and can add additional ones. In Suggestions for Further Reading (see page 123), we identify some books you can read to learn more about grammar, but the important message of this book is to make grammar a focus of attention and discussion in the classroom as often as you can. Engage your students in discovering and talking about form–meaning connections and you will find that the metalanguage becomes a useful resource for learning.

Conclusion

In this book, we have seen that the curriculum expectations for growth in content learning across the years of schooling provide teachers with important information about what the focus of their grammar teaching should be. By recognizing what learners need to do with language across subject areas, and then highlighting how language works to support those objectives, teachers enable students to learn the forms and meanings of the target language. Looking closely at language–meaning connections helps L2 learners better understand how the language they are learning works to make meanings. The ideas presented in this book offer a framework for connecting language forms and meaning in contexts of use, recognizing grammar as a resource that supports L2 learners in developing their meaning-making repertoires.

This book introduced functional grammar as an approach to teaching grammar that is explicit in its focus on language and in linking form and meaning. As discussed in Chapter 2, the key theoretical principle underlying this approach is the idea that when we use language, we are simultaneously presenting ideas, enacting a relationship with the listener or reader, and constructing a cohesive message. As we saw throughout the book, each of these three angles can be addressed in grammar instruction.

To present ideas, we focus on the content of the message and on the information contributed by participants, processes, circumstances, and connectors. We have reviewed some of the research that shows how L2 learners can analyze sentences, using this metalanguage to recognize the meaningful phrases that together construct meanings in sentences and texts.

In every use of language, we enact relationships with the reader or listener. In this book, you saw examples of how teachers explored the ways different grammatical choices support different kinds of interaction and exchange of meanings through a focus on mood and speech function. We can be formal or informal, close or distant, and include various kinds of attitudes. Different grammatical choices enable these different interactional stances.

We also explored how a cohesive message that holds together and builds from clause to clause is constructed in the grammar. For example, we looked at connectors that build relationships between parts of the clause or text, and reference that is constructed in cohesive ties presented in pronouns, demonstratives, and synonyms, among other linguistic resources.

Of course, these particular grammatical systems are only a subset of the grammar of English or any other language. Exploring grammar is engaging and fun for children when done with a focus on meaning, and many other grammatical systems can also be a source of exploration and engagement in the classroom.

Regardless of whether learners are in primary or secondary school, we have seen that grammar teaching plays a vital role in language learning. Throughout our discussion of grammar instruction in primary and secondary classrooms, we have shown how thinking about Gibbons' four moves can help you embed grammar teaching in a unit of instruction. You can highlight the grammar in focus, provide models of the way it is used in different texts and tasks, and support learners in using it by reminding and handing over. We saw that movement back and forth across the mode continuum is important for allowing L2 students to draw on what they can already do with language as they move from face-to-face interaction into retelling experience, reporting on what they have learned, and writing texts appropriate to different school subjects and genres. In Chapters 3 and 4, we saw how the pedagogical moves used to support this movement can be integrated and used in classroom instruction.

This book has presented many ways of making grammar instruction engaging and meaningful both for you and for your L2 learners. We hope that the ideas we propose encourage you to make the most of grammar instruction by focusing on grammar and meaning.

Suggestions for Further Reading

Below we list books about grammar teaching and learning that you may find useful. Not all are specific to school-age learners, but all provide valuable background for understanding grammar for learning language and using grammar to learn other subjects in school.

Butt, D., Fahey, R., Feez, S., & Spinks, S. (2012). *Using functional grammar: An explorer's guide, third edition*. South Yarra, Victoria: Palgrave Macmillan.

This book is a great resource for students and teachers of English as a first, second, or foreign language. The authors start out by introducing basic concepts of traditional grammar. They then discuss language in context and text types, and explore functional grammar in more detail. The book also includes practical applications of functional grammar theory for language education and provides examples of multimodal analysis of texts.

Celce-Murcia, M., & Larsen-Freeman, D. (1998). *The grammar book: An ESL/EFL teacher's course, second edition*. Boston, MA: Heinle & Heinle.

Celce-Murcia and Larsen-Freeman's book is widely used in teacher education programs and helps teachers and future teachers of ESL/EFL understand English grammar and the linguistic system. The book is divided into sections that deal with form, meaning, and use. While not focusing on functional grammar, this book provides a good introduction to the traditional grammar system.

Christie, F. (2012). Language education throughout the school years: A functional perspective. [Language Learning Monograph Series]. *Language Learning, 62* (Supplement 1).

This book offers a way of thinking about what grammar can be in focus at different grade levels, in different content areas, and for writing different genres across the years of schooling.

Coffin, C., Donohue, J., & North, S. (2009). *Exploring English grammar: From formal to functional.* London: Routledge.

   This is a valuable resource that bridges traditional and functional grammar. The authors start with a traditional approach and expand traditional tools for analysis to incorporate functional grammar. The book explores how grammatical structures function in different contexts and focuses on real-world issues in accessible activities to help readers analyze formal and functional grammar in different genres and styles.

Derewianka, B. (2011). *A new grammar companion for teachers.* Sydney: Primary English Teachers Association.

   Derewianka's book is a useful resource to familiarize teachers with the basics of the English grammatical system. Presenting grammatical categories organized according to how they construct meaning in context, this book uses traditional grammatical terminology along with functional metalanguage to expand teachers' understanding of grammar as a resource.

Fang, Z., & Schleppegrell, M. J. (2008). *Reading in secondary content areas: A language-based pedagogy.* Ann Arbor, MI: University of Michigan Press.

   This book presents a functional grammar approach to teaching reading in different content areas. Fang, Schleppegrell, and the other contributors to the book address the specialized knowledge and contexts for learning that are relevant to secondary classrooms in history, mathematics, science, and Language Arts. This book provides many examples of how functional grammar can be applied to address the abstract, technical, and hierarchically organized language of the secondary content areas.

Gibbons, P. (2002). *Scaffolding language, scaffolding learning: Teaching second language learners in the mainstream classroom.* Portsmouth, NH: Heinemann.

   Gibbons shows how to integrate the teaching of English with the content areas for ESL students at the elementary school level. This book combines Vygotsky's sociocultural theories of learning with Halliday's functional model of language applied to second language learning. The teaching and learning activities provide excellent examples that teachers can use to scaffold language and learning in the content areas.

Gibbons, P. (2009). *English learners, academic literacy, and thinking: Learning in the challenge zone.* Portsmouth, NH: Heinemann.

Focusing on developing high-challenge, high-support classrooms, Gibbons presents a literacy-based approach for ESL students at the middle school level. She integrates conceptual understanding, critical thinking, content area knowledge, and academic literacy into content-based instruction. She addresses reading, writing, classroom talk, and academic listening, and presents guidelines for designing high-quality instruction through helpful activities and tasks for ESL students.

Jones, R. H., & Lock, G. (2011). *Functional grammar in the ESL classroom: Noticing, exploring and practising.* Basingstoke: Palgrave Macmillan.

This book introduces functional grammar for students to focus on both form and meaning, providing techniques to see how grammar works in real-world contexts. Jones and Lock include many different grammatical topics such as verb tense, voice, reference, and the organization of texts.

Lock, G. (1996). *Functional English grammar: An introduction for second language teachers.* Cambridge: Cambridge University Press.

Each chapter of this introduction to functional grammar focuses on areas of difficulty for L2 learners, providing examples of how the grammar feature functions in different genres, tasks for engagement in grammatical analysis, and discussion questions about meaning and structure. The book is a valuable resource for teachers who want to understand the nature of English grammar from a functional perspective and get ideas for teaching features that are problematic for L2 learners.

Locke, T. (Ed.). (2010). *Beyond the grammar wars: A resource for teachers and students on developing language knowledge in the English/literacy classroom.* New York, NY: Routledge.

This collection of chapters provides a historical overview of the debates around grammar and English/literacy teaching in the United States, England, Scotland, and Australia. Examples of grammar-based approaches are described and their effectiveness in English/literacy classrooms is discussed. The volume provides activities that enable readers to apply the content of the book to their own teaching contexts.

Glossary

academic language: the vocabulary, sentence patterns, text organization, and style of speaking/writing used in educational or professional environments. Also known as 'the language of schooling' (Schleppegrell, 2004).

agency: the degree to which an entity is presented as an active agent, rather than being acted upon.

circumstance: a functional grammar term referring to the prepositional phrase and adverb group; the *when, where, how,* and *why* of the process.

coherence: the way in which a text holds together through links in meanings within the text and in a larger context.

cohesion: the way in which a text holds together through grammatical and lexical features which link one part of the text with another.

communicative language teaching approaches: language as communication; meaning and use are of utmost importance.

complex noun groups: noun phrases that present abstract and theoretical knowledge in dense constructions with a noun and its modifiers and embedded clauses.

comprehensible input: language that a listener/reader can understand. Krashen (1982) hypothesized that L2 acquisition occurs when L2 listeners/readers are exposed to language they can understand.

comprehensible output: a term used by Swain (1985) to make the point that when learners have to produce language in speech or writing, they have to attend to form and subsequently move towards greater proficiency.

conjunction: a type of function word that connects clauses and builds relationships between parts of the clause or text.

connector: refers to the conjunctions and other linking phrases that create cohesion and a logical development across a text.

content: the information and ways of thinking that students are expected to acquire and retain about subject matter such as history, science, mathematics, and literature.

Content and Language Integrated Learning (CLIL): an approach to learning an L2 that focuses on teaching both the language and the content.

corrective feedback: a response to a learner's error (or incorrect performance), informal or formal, verbal or written.

declarative: a mood choice typically used to make statements.

deconstruct: to analyze a text into its meaningful parts in order to study both language and meaning.

English Language Learner (ELL): a term often used in the US context to describe an L2 learner of English.

explicit instruction: instruction that draws overt attention to grammatical form (as opposed to implicit instruction, in which exemplars of grammatical features are present without any reference to rules).

feedback: information that tells speakers or writers whether what they have said or written has been understood and, sometimes, whether it is accurate and appropriate.

first language: the language that was acquired first in a person's life. Also referred to as 'home language'.

foreign language (FL): a language that is not ordinarily spoken among people in a learner's local environment.

form-focused instruction: instruction that draws attention to language form embedded within communicative language teaching.

functional grammar instruction: starting with the work by Michael Halliday, instruction that focuses on meaning and draws attention to the contexts in which language is used.

genre: a set of texts, written or spoken, associated with the same social purpose.

grammar: the full set of language resources, or patterns of language, through which meaning is presented, created, and shared.

immersion: a program of instruction in a second or foreign language that uses only the target language as the medium of instruction.

imperative: a mood choice typically used for commands.

incidental focus on form: occurs spontaneously within communicative activities.

interrogative: a mood choice typically used for questions.

L1: see 'first language'.

L2: see 'second language' and 'foreign language'.

Language Arts: the term used in the USA to refer to what in other contexts might be called 'subject English'; instruction in language and literature.

language variation: refers to the way language varies according to context of use, whether as dialect variation or register variation.

lexical: having to do with vocabulary.

literacy: the ability to read, write, and understand language in a variety of contexts, especially those requiring knowledge of academic language.

metalanguage: a language for talking about language. There is traditional metalanguage (for example, *verb*, *noun*, and *adjective*), but this book also highlights the importance of functional metalanguage (for example, *participant*, *process*, and *connector*), which more closely relates form and meaning.

metatalk: Swain and Lapkin's (2002) term, which refers to conscious reflection on language through collaborative conversations.

modality: the language system that expresses degrees of certainty, obligation, ability, and usuality.

mode continuum: Gibbons' (2006a) term, which refers to the movement between spoken and written language, as well as between more everyday and more technical language.

mood: the interpersonal grammatical systems for presenting different speech functions; grammatical systems that present clauses as imperative, interrogative, or declarative.

morphology: the study of morphemes, the smallest structural units that have meanings in words.

nominalization: occurs when a process is presented grammatically as a noun.

noticing: a term used to refer to a specific mental action for second language acquisition. Noticing promotes students' consciousness about the linguistic choices they can make when engaged in meaning-making tasks.

participant: a functional grammar term referring to a noun group; who or what is participating in the process, represented as person(s) or thing(s).

pedagogical moves: this term is used by Gibbons (2006a) to refer to the four ways in which students move across the mode continuum in order to expand their meaning-making resources. The four moves are: 'talking about language, using meaningful metalanguage'; 'unpacking written language'; 'recasting student discourse'; and 'reminding and handing over'.

planned focus on form: involves planning for instruction and attention to a particular grammatical structure.

proactive focus on form: planned in advance to help learners focus on language as they listen, speak, read, and write.

process: a functional grammar term referring to the verb group; shows what is going on (the *doing, thinking, saying,* or *being*).

proficiency: the level or ability an individual has in using a language.

reactive focus on form: responding to learners' errors, in either speech or writing, typically by providing feedback.

recast: a type of feedback that reformulates the learner's error and models the correct form. For Gibbons (2006a), recasting is responding to student-initiated topics by restating their contributions in more authoritative, technical, or disciplinary discourse.

reference: constructed in cohesive ties presented in pronouns, demonstratives, and synonyms, among other linguistic resources.

register: a variety of language which is distinguished by its context of use, or by the situation in which it is used.

scaffolding: temporary support given to the learner during the learning process in order to best facilitate learning.

second language (L2): a language learned after the first language (L1) has been acquired.

sentence combining: a method which encourages students to put ideas together to create more complex sentences.

sheltered instruction: teaching that is adapted to the needs of L2 learners, employing pedagogical strategies and materials that allow L2 learners to access academic content appropriate for their age level.

SLA (second language acquisition): both the process by which an individual learns a second language, and the actual study of that process.

sociolinguistic competence: the ability to use language in a socially appropriate manner.

speech function: an interpersonal semantic system through which we state, question, offer, or command.

syntactic structures: ways in which words, phrases, and clauses are constructed and combined in sentences.

systemic functional linguistics (SFL): Michael Halliday's linguistic theory that offers a framework for connecting language forms and meaning in contexts of use and for viewing grammar as a meaning-making resource.

traditional grammar instruction: involves learning rules for correctness and applying them.

References

Achugar, M., Schleppegrell, M. J., & Oteíza, T. (2007). Engaging teachers in language analysis: A functional linguistics approach to reflective literacy. *English Teaching: Practice and Critique*, *6*, 8–24.

Aguirre-Muñoz, Z., Park, J.-E., Amabisca, A., & Boscardin, C. K. (2008). Developing teacher capacity for serving ELLs' writing instructional needs: A case for systemic functional linguistics. *Bilingual Research Journal*, *31*, 1–28.

Bailey, A. L., & Heritage, M. (2008). *Formative assessment for literacy, grades K–6: Building reading and academic language skills across the curriculum.* Thousand Oaks, CA: Corwin/Sage Press.

Bash, B. (1990). *Urban roosts: Where birds nest in the city.* Boston, MA: Little, Brown.

Beck, R. B., Black, L., Krieger, L. S., Naylor, P. C., & Shabaka, D. I. (2003). *Modern world history: Patterns of interaction.* Evanston, IL: McDougal Littell.

Berry, R. (2005). Making the most of metalanguage. *Language Awareness*, *14*, 13–18.

Berry, R. (2010). *Terminology in English language teaching: Nature and use.* Bern: Peter Lang.

Boehm, R., Hoone, C., McGowan, T., McKinney-Browning, M., Miramontes, O., & Porter, P. (2000). *California.* Orlando, FL: Harcourt Brace.

Butt, D., Fahey, R., Feez, S., & Spinks, S. (2012). *Using functional grammar: An explorer's guide, third edition.* South Yarra, Victoria: Palgrave Macmillan.

California Department of Education (2001). *History-Social science framework for California public schools.* Sacramento, CA.

Cayton, A., Perry, E. I., Reed, L., & Winkler, A. M. (2002). *America: Pathways to the present.* Upper Saddle River, NJ: Prentice Hall.

Celce-Murcia, M., & Larsen-Freeman, D. (1998). *The grammar book: An ESL/EFL teacher's course, second edition.* Boston, MA: Heinle & Heinle.

Chapin, S. H., O'Connor, C., & Anderson, N. C. (2003). *Classroom discussions: Using math talk to help students learn.* Sausalito, CA: Math Solutions Publishers.

Christie, F. (2012). Language education throughout the school years: A functional perspective. [Language Learning Monograph Series]. *Language Learning*, *62* (Supplement 1).

Christie, F., & Derewianka, B. (2010). *School discourse: Learning to write across the years of schooling.* London: Continuum.

Coffin, C., Donohue, J., & North, S. (2009). *Exploring English grammar: From formal to functional.* London: Routledge.

Cummins, J., & Man, E. Y. (2007). Academic language: What is it and how do we acquire it? In J. Cummins & C. Davison (Eds.), *International handbook of English language teaching* (Vol. II, pp. 797–810). New York, NY: Springer.

Dare, B. (2010). Learning about language: The role of metalanguage. *NALDIC Quarterly*, 8, 18–25.

de Oliveira, L. C. (2010). Nouns in history: Packaging information, expanding explanations, and structuring reasoning. *The History Teacher*, 43, 191–203.

de Oliveira, L. C. (2011). *Knowing and writing school history: The language of students' expository writing and teachers' expectations*. Charlotte, NC: Information Age Publishing.

de Oliveira, L. C. (2012). What history teachers need to know about academic language to teach English language learners. *The Social Studies Review*, 51, 76–9.

de Oliveira, L. C., & Dodds, K. N. (2010). Beyond general strategies for English Language Learners: Language dissection in science. *The Electronic Journal of Literacy Through Science*, 9, 1–14. Retrieved July 21 2014 from http://ejlts.ucdavis.edu/article/2010/9/1/beyond-general-strategies-english-language-learners-language-dissection-science

de Oliveira, L. C., & Lan, S.-W. (2014). Writing science in an upper elementary classroom: A genre-based approach to teaching English language learners. *Journal of Second Language Writing*, 25, 23–39.

de Oliveira, L. C., Lan, S.-W., & Dodds, K. (2013). Reading, writing, and talking science with English language learners. In J. Nagle (Ed.), *English learner instruction through collaboration and inquiry in teacher education* (pp. 3–23). Charlotte, NC: Information Age Publishing.

Derewianka, B. (2011). *A new grammar companion for teachers*. Sydney: Primary English Teachers Association.

Doughty, C., & Varela, E. (1998). Communicative focus on form. In C. Doughty & J. Williams (Eds.), *Focus on form in classroom second language acquisition* (pp. 114–138). Cambridge: Cambridge University Press.

Doughty, C., & Williams, J. (Eds.). (1998). *Focus on form in classroom second language acquisition*. Cambridge: Cambridge University Press.

Droga, L., & Humphrey, S. (2003). *Grammar and meaning: An introduction for primary teachers*. Berry, NSW: Target Texts.

Ellis, N. (2005). At the interface: How explicit knowledge affects implicit language learning. *Studies in Second Language Acquisition*, 27, 305–52.

Ellis, N., & Larsen-Freeman, D. (2006). Language emergence: Implications for applied linguistics–Introduction to the special issue. *Applied Linguistics*, 27, 558–89.

Ellis, R. (2001). Investigating form-focused instruction. *Language Learning*, 51, 1–46.

Ellis, R. (2002). The place of grammar instruction in the second/foreign language curriculum. In E. Hinkel & S. Fotos (Eds.), *New perspectives on grammar teaching in second language classrooms* (pp. 17–34). Mahwah, NJ: Erlbaum.

Ellis, R. (2006). Current issues in the teaching of grammar: An SLA perspective. *TESOL Quarterly*, 40, 83–107.

Ellis, R., Basturkmen, H., & Loewen, S. (2002). Doing focus-on-form. *System*, 30, 419–32.

European Commission. (1995). *Teaching and learning: Towards the learning society. White paper on education and training.* COM (95) 590. Brussels.

Fang, Z., & Schleppegrell, M. J. (2008). *Reading in secondary content areas: A language-based pedagogy.* Ann Arbor, MI: University of Michigan Press.

French, R. (2010). Primary school children learning grammar: Rethinking the possibilities. In T. Locke (Ed.), *Beyond the grammar wars: A resource for teachers and students on developing language knowledge in the English/literacy classroom* (pp. 206–29). New York: Routledge.

French, R. (2012). Learning the grammatics of quoted speech: Benefits for punctuation and expressive reading. *Australian Journal of Language and Literacy, 35,* 206–22.

Frey, W. (2005). *History alive! The medieval world and beyond.* Palo Alto, CA: Teachers' Curriculum Institute.

Gebhard, M., Harman, R., & Seger, W. (2007). Reclaiming recess in urban schools: The potential of systemic functional linguistics for ELLs and their teachers. *Language Arts, 84,* 419–30.

Gebhard, M., Chen, I.-A., Graham, H., & Gunawan, W. (2013). Teaching to mean, writing to mean: SFL, L2 literacy, and teacher education. *Journal of Second Language Writing, 22,* 107–24.

Genesee, F. (1987). *Learning through two languages: Studies of immersion and bilingual education.* Rowley, MA: Newbury House.

Gibbons, P. (1998). Classroom talk and the learning of new registers in a second language. *Language and Education, 12,* 99–118.

Gibbons, P. (2002). *Scaffolding language, scaffolding learning: Teaching second language learners in the mainstream classroom.* Portsmouth, NH: Heinemann.

Gibbons, P. (2003). Mediating language learning: Teacher interactions with ESL students in a content-based classroom. *TESOL Quarterly, 37,* 247–73.

Gibbons, P. (2006a). *Bridging discourses in the ESL classroom: Students, teachers and researchers.* New York: Continuum.

Gibbons, P. (2006b). Steps for planning an integrated program for ESL learners in mainstream classes. In P. McKay (Ed.), *Planning and teaching creatively within a required curriculum for school-age learners* (pp. 215–33). Alexandria, VA: TESOL.

Gibbons, P. (2008). 'It was taught good and I learned a lot': Intellectual practices and ESL learners in the middle years. *Australian Journal of Language and Literacy, 31,* 155–73.

Gibbons, P. (2009). *English learners, academic literacy, and thinking: Learning in the challenge zone.* Portsmouth, NH: Heinemann.

Godley, A. J., Sweetland, J., Wheeler, R. S., Minnici, A., & Carpenter, B. D. (2006). Preparing teachers for dialectally diverse classrooms. *Educational Researcher, 35,* 30–7.

Halliday, M. A. K. (1978). *Language as social semiotic. The social interpretation of language and meaning.* London: Edward Arnold.

Halliday, M. A. K. (1994). *An introduction to functional grammar, second edition.* London: Edward Arnold.

Halliday, M. A. K. (2004). Three aspects of children's language development: Learning language, learning through language, learning about language (1980). In J. Webster (Ed.), *The language of early childhood* (Vol. 4, pp. 308–26). London: Continuum.

Harley, B. (1998). The role of focus-on-form tasks in promoting child L2 acquisition. In C. Doughty & J. Williams (Eds.), *Focus on form in classroom second language acquisition* (pp. 156–74). New York: Cambridge University Press.

Harley, B., Cummins, J., Swain, M., & Allen, P. (1990). The nature of language proficiency. In B. Harley, P. Allen, J. Cummins, & M. Swain (Eds.), *The development of second language proficiency* (pp. 7–25). Cambridge: Cambridge University Press.

Harley, B., & Swain, M. (1984). The interlanguage of immersion students and its implications for second language teaching. In A. Davies, C. Criper, & A. Howatt (Eds.), *Interlanguage* (pp. 291–311). Edinburgh: Edinburgh University Press.

Humphrey, S., Droga, L., & Feez, S. (2012). *Grammar and meaning*. Sydney: Primary English Teaching Association.

Janzen, J. (2007). Preparing teachers of second language reading. *TESOL Quarterly, 41*, 707–29.

Johnson, A. (1993). *Julius*. New York, NY: Orchard Books.

Jones, R. H., & Lock, G. (2011). *Functional grammar in the ESL classroom: Noticing, exploring and practising*. Basingstoke: Palgrave Macmillan.

Krashen, S. (1982). *Principles and practice in second language acquisition*. Oxford: Pergamon Press.

Lightbown, P. (2014). *Focus on content-based language teaching*. Oxford: Oxford University Press.

Lightbown, P., & Spada, N. (2013). *How languages are learned, fourth edition*. Oxford: Oxford University Press.

Lindholm-Leary, K., & Borsato, G. (2006). Academic achievement. In F. Genesee, K. Lindholm-Leary, W. M. Saunders, & D. Christian (Eds.), *Educating English language learners: A synthesis of research evidence* (pp. 176–222). New York, NY: Cambridge University Press.

Llinares, A., Morton, T., & Whittaker, R. (2012). *The roles of language in CLIL*. Cambridge: Cambridge University Press.

Llinares, A., & Whittaker, R. (2010). Writing and speaking in the history class: A comparative analysis of CLIL and first language contexts. In C. Dalton-Puffer, T. Nikula, & U. Smit (Eds.), *Language use and language learning in CLIL classrooms* (pp. 125–43). Amsterdam: John Benjamins.

Lock, G. (1996). *Functional English grammar: An introduction for second language teachers*. Cambridge: Cambridge University Press.

Locke, T. (Ed.). (2010). *Beyond the grammar wars: A resource for teachers and students on developing language knowledge in the English/literacy classroom*. New York, NY: Routledge.

Lyster, R. (2004). Differential effects of prompts and recasts in form-focused instruction. *Studies in Second Language Acquisition, 26*, 399–432.

Lyster, R. (2007). *Learning and teaching languages through content: A counterbalanced approach*. Herndon, VA: John Benjamins.

Lyster, R., & Ranta, L. (1997). Corrective feedback and learner uptake. *Studies in Second Language Acquisition, 19*, 37–66.

Macken-Horarik, M. (1996). Literacy and learning across the curriculum: Towards a model of register for secondary school teachers. In R. Hasan, & G. Williams, *Literacy in society* (pp. 124–71). London: Longman.

Martin, J. R., & Rose, D. (2003). *Working with discourse: Meaning beyond the clause, first edition.* London: Continuum.

Moore, J., & Schleppegrell, M. J. (2014). Using a functional linguistics metalanguage to support academic language development in the English Language Arts. *Linguistics and Education, 26*, 92–105.

Myhill, D. (2003). Principled understanding? Teaching the active and passive voice. *Language and Education, 17*, 355–70.

Nassaji, H., & Fotos, S. (2004). Current developments in research on the teaching of grammar. *Annual Review of Applied Linguistics, 24*, 126–45.

Norris, J. M., & Ortega, L. (2000). Effectiveness of L2 instruction: A research synthesis and quantitative meta-analysis. *Language Learning, 5*, 417–528.

Norris, J. M., & Ortega, L. (2009). Towards an organic approach to investigating CAF in instructed SLA: The case of complexity. *Applied Linguistics, 30*, 555–78.

Oliver, R., & Philp, J. (2014). *Focus on oral interaction.* Oxford: Oxford University Press.

Rathmann, P. (1995). *Officer Buckle and Gloria.* New York, NY: Putnam Juvenile.

Rose, D., & Martin, J. R. (2012). *Learning to write, reading to learn: Genre, knowledge and pedagogy in the Sydney school.* London: Equinox.

Schleppegrell, M. J. (2004). *The language of schooling: A functional linguistics perspective.* Mahwah, NJ: Erbaum.

Schleppegrell, M. J. (2013). The role of metalanguage in supporting academic language development. *Language Learning, 63*, 153–70.

Schleppegrell, M. J., & Achugar, M. (2003). Learning language and learning history: A functional linguistics approach. *TESOL Journal, 12*, 21–7.

Schleppegrell, M. J., Achugar, M., & Oteíza, T. (2004). The grammar of history: Enhancing content-based instruction through a functional focus on language. *TESOL Quarterly, 38*, 67–93.

Schleppegrell, M. J., & de Oliveira, L. C. (2006). An integrated language and content approach for history teachers. *Journal of English for Academic Purposes, 5*, 254–68.

Schleppegrell, M. J., Greer, S., & Taylor, S. (2008). Literacy in history: Language and meaning. *Australian Journal of Language and Literacy, 31*, 174–87.

Schleppegrell, M. J., & O'Hallaron, C. L. (2011). Teaching academic language in L2 secondary settings. *Annual Review of Applied Linguistics, 31*, 3–18.

Schmidt, R. (1990). The role of consciousness in second language learning. *Applied Linguistics, 11*, 129–58.

Scott Foresman Science (2006). Grade 4. Upper Saddle River, NJ: Pearson Scott Foresman. Retrieved July 21 2014 from http://pearsonkt.com/summaryStreetOT/texts/Sci-National-Grade-4/iText/products/0-328-34278-5/i.html

Shin, S. J. (2009). Negotiating grammatical choices: Academic language learning by secondary ESL students. *System, 37*, 391–402.

Simard, D., & Jean, G. (2011). An exploration of L2 teachers' use of pedagogical interventions devised to draw L2 learners' attention to form. *Language Learning, 61,* 759–85.

Snow, M. A. (1998). Trends and issues in content-based instruction. *Annual Review of Applied Linguistics, 18,* 243–67.

Snow, M. A., Met, M., & Genesee, F. (1989). A conceptual framework for the integration of language and content in second/foreign language instruction. *TESOL Quarterly, 23,* 201–17. Reprinted in P. A. Richard-Amato, & M. A. Snow (Eds.), (1992). *The multicultural classroom: Readings for content-area teachers* (pp. 27–38). Reading, MA: Addison-Wesley.

Spada, N. (2010). Beyond form-focused instruction: Reflections on past, present and future research. *Language Teaching, 44,* 225–36.

Spada, N., & Lightbown, P. M. (1993). Instruction and the development of questions in L2 classrooms. *Studies in Second Language Acquisition, 15,* 205–24.

Spada, N., & Lightbown, P. M. (1999). Instruction, L1 influence and developmental readiness in second language acquisition. *Modern Language Journal, 83,* 1–22.

Spycher, P. (2007). Academic writing of adolescent English learners: Learning to use 'although'. *Journal of Second Language Writing, 16,* 238–54.

Svalberg, A. M.-L. (2007). Language awareness and language learning. *Language Teaching, 40,* 287–308.

Swain, M. (1985). Communicative competence: Some roles of comprehensible input and comprehensible output in its development. In S. Gass & C. G. Madden (Eds.), *Input in second language acquisition* (pp. 235–53). Rowley, MA: Newbury House.

Swain, M. (1995). Three functions of output in second language learning. In G. Cook & B. Seidlhofer (Eds.), *Principle and practice in applied linguistics: Studies in honour of H. G. Widdowson* (pp. 125–44). Oxford: Oxford University Press.

Swain, M. (1996). Integrating language and content in immersion classrooms: Research perspectives. *The Canadian Modern Language Review, 52,* 529–48.

Swain, M., & Lapkin, S. (2002). Talking it through: Two French immersion learners' response to reformulation. *International Journal of Educational Research, 37,* 285–304.

Vygotsky, L. (1978). *Mind in Society.* Cambridge, MA: Harvard University Press.

Vygotsky, L. (1986). *Thought and language.* Cambridge, MA: MIT Press.

Wajnryb, R. (1990). *Grammar dictation.* Oxford: Oxford University Press.

Wells, G. (Ed.). (1994). *Changing schools from within: Creating communities of inquiry.* Portsmouth, NH: Heinemann.

Wells, G. (1999). *Dialogic inquiry: Towards a socio-cultural practice and theory of education.* Cambridge: Cambridge University Press.

Whittaker, R. (2010). Using systemic-functional linguistics in content and language integrated learning. *NALDIC Quarterly, 8,* 31–6.

Whittaker, R., & Llinares, A. (2009). CLIL in social science classrooms: Analysis of spoken and written productions. In Y. Ruiz de Zarobe & R. M. Jiménez Catalán (Eds.), *Content and language integrated learning: Evidence from research in Europe.* (pp. 215–34). London: Multilingual Matters.

Williams, G. (2004). Ontogenesis and grammatics: Functions of metalanguage in pedagogical discourse. In G. Williams & A. Lukin (Eds.), *The development of language: Functional perspectives on species and individuals* (pp. 241–67). London: Continuum.

Williams, G. (2005). Grammatics in schools. In R. Hasan, C. M. I. M. Matthiessen, & J. Webster (Eds.), *Continuing discourse on language* (pp. 281–310). London: Equinox.

Zyzik, E., & Polio, C. (2008). Incidental focus on form in Spanish literature courses. *The Modern Language Journal, 92,* 50–73.

Index

Page numbers annotated with 'g' and 't' refer to glossary entries and tables respectively.